DISCOVERING OU

A HISTORY OF THE UNITED STA

MW01256432

CHAPTER TESTS
& LESSON QUIZZES

Mc
Graw
Hill
Education

networks

DISCOVERING OUR PAST
A HISTORY OF THE UNITED STATES, EARLY YEARS

mheducation.com/prek-12

Send all inquiries to:
McGraw-Hill Education
8787 Orion Place
Columbus, OH 43240

IISBN: 978-0-07-676633-8
MHID: 0-07-676633-0

Printed in the United States of America.

3 4 5 6 7 8 9 LHS 23 22 21 20 19 18

Table of Contents

Table of Contents continued

Table of Contents continued

Table of Contents continued

Lesson Quiz 1-1

netw🌐rks

The First Americans

DIRECTIONS: Matching Match each item with its definition.

_____ **1.** a person who moves from place to place

_____ **2.** an object left behind by early peoples

_____ **3.** a narrow passage of water connecting two larger bodies of water

_____ **4.** the study of the material remains of ancient peoples

_____ **5.** the movement of a large number of people to a new area

A. archaeology

B. artifact

C. migration

D. nomad

E. strait

DIRECTIONS: Multiple Choice Indicate the answer choice that best answers the question.

_____ **6.** Which of these is a type of corn?

    A. bison   **C.** squash

    B. maize   **D.** wheat

_____ **7.** Which of these was a land bridge from another continent to North America?

    A. Alaska   **C.** Beringia

    B. Atlantic Ocean   **D.** Bering Strait

_____ **8.** Why did ancient people probably first come to the Americas?

    A. to plant and harvest crops

    B. to hunt animals for food

    C. to seek religious freedom

    D. to find trading partners

_____ **9.** Which of these animals was a food source for early Americans?

    A. lions   **C.** mastodons

    B. maize   **D.** tigers

_____ **10.** Where do many archaeologists believe the earliest Americans came from?

    A. Asia   **C.** North America

    B. England   **D.** South America

Discovering Our Past: A History of the United States

Lesson Quiz 1-2

networks

The First Americans

DIRECTIONS: True/False Indicate whether the statement is true or false.

_____ **1.** The Olmec built stone houses, monuments, and drainage systems.

_____ **2.** The Maya developed a type of writing called Malinche.

_____ **3.** The Inca kept records by using quipus.

_____ **4.** The Aztec capital of Tenochtitlán was also known as Pachacuti.

_____ **5.** The Olmec had little influence on the civilizations that came afterward.

DIRECTIONS: Multiple Choice Indicate the answer choice that best answers the question.

_____ **6.** Which of these was a distinguishing feature of Inca farming?

    A. the use of terraces

    B. the use of calendars

    C. the use of hieroglyphics

    D. the use of rope

_____ **7.** What is a society run by religious leaders called?

    A. a civilization   **C.** a culture

    B. a democracy   **D.** a theocracy

_____ **8.** Which was an Aztec city that was once the largest in the Americas?

    A. Chichén Itzá   **C.** Tenochtitlán

    B. Mexico City   **D.** Yucatán

_____ **9.** Which of these was a way the Maya used their temples?

    A. grain storage

    B. governmental centers

    C. guest houses

    D. throne rooms

_____ **10.** Which early American civilization was the largest?

    A. Aztec   **C.** Maya

    B. Inca   **D.** Olmec

Lesson Quiz 1-3

networks

The First Americans

DIRECTIONS: Completion Enter the appropriate word(s) to complete the statement.

1. The place where Utah, Colorado, Arizona, and New Mexico meet is today called _____.

2. The Inuit lived in the _____ region of North America.

3. The peoples of the Southwest used sun-dried mud called _____ to construct their buildings.

4. The Iroquois Constitution established a ruling body called the _____.

DIRECTIONS: Multiple Choice Indicate the answer choice that best completes the statement or answers the question.

_____ 5. Which group of native peoples is known for its extensive irrigation systems?

    A. Anasazi

    B. Hohokam

    C. Mississippians

    D. Mound Builders

_____ 6. Which Native American group made warm, waterproof clothing from seal skin?

    A. Chinook

    B. Haida

    C. Inuit

    D. Nez Perce

_____ 7. In which of these groups did women play a strong role in the government?

    A. Iroquois League

    B. Mohawk Nation

    C. Native American Federation

    D. Oneida Nation

_____ 8. By what name is Illinois's largest earthworks complex known?

    A. Cahokia

    B. Mesa Verde

    C. Pueblo Bonito

    D. Seneca

Chapter 1 Test, Traditional

networks

The First Americans

DIRECTIONS: True/False Indicate whether the statement is true or false.

_____ **1.** The Maya were the first Americans to use horses and wheeled carts.

_____ **2.** Archaeologists do not know the exact date when the first people appeared in North America.

_____ **3.** Some early Americans hunted bison and mammoths.

_____ **4.** The Anasazi built mud-brick dwellings called mounds.

_____ **5.** The Cherokee lived in the northernmost region of North America.

DIRECTIONS: Matching Match each item with its definition.

_____ **6.** group of related families

_____ **7.** a building

_____ **8.** a scientific way to determine the age of an artifact

_____ **9.** highly detailed

_____ **10.** a rough calculation of a number

A. clan

B. carbon dating

C. complex

D. structure

E. estimate

DIRECTIONS: Multiple Choice Indicate the answer choice that best answers the question.

_____ **11.** The first Native Americans probably reached North America by crossing which of the following?

    A. Alaskan Sea

    B. Bering Strait

    C. Atlantic Ocean

    D. Pacific Ocean

_____ **12.** Which of these resulted from the Maya's study of astronomy?

    A. 365-day calendar

    B. colorful cave paintings

    C. the first globe

    D. discovery of Neptune

_____ **13.** People in which American region made use of tepees?

    A. North

    B. Plains

    C. Southwest

    D. West

_____ **14.** Who chose the male members of the Iroquois Grand Council?

    A. male members

    B. group mothers

    C. clan mothers

    D. all the people

_____ **15.** Which of these Native American groups relied on salmon as a main food source?

    A. Chinook

    B. Cherokee

    C. Apache

    D. Plains peoples

> "Motecuhzoma [leader of the Aztec, also known as Montezuma] now arrayed himself in his finery. . . . The other great princes also adorned their persons. . . . They all went out together to meet the strangers. They brought trays heaped with the finest flowers—the flower that resembles a shield; the flower shaped like a heart; in the center, the flower with the sweetest aroma. . . . They also brought garlands of flowers, and ornaments for the breast, and necklaces of gold, necklaces hung with rich stones."
>
> —*The Broken Spears: The Aztec Account of the Conquest of Mexico*

_____ **16.** This eyewitness account tells of the first European visit to the city of Tenochtitlán. According to the account, how were the Spaniards received?

    A. The Aztec ambushed them.

    B. The Aztec greeted them as honored visitors.

    C. The Aztec fled their city in terror.

    D. The Aztec drove them from Tenochtitlán.

_____ **17.** Which of these descriptions from the passage above indicates the Aztec response to the Spaniards' visit?

    A. Aztec hiding places

    B. Aztec weapons

    C. Aztec flowers and necklaces

    D. Aztec children crying

Chapter 1 Test, Traditional *cont.*

networks

> "The [Aztec] messengers also said [to Montezuma]: 'Their trappings and arms are all made of iron. They dress in iron and wear iron casques on their heads. Their swords are iron; their bows are iron; their shields are iron; their spears are iron. Their deer carry them on their backs wherever they wish to go. These deer, our lord, are as tall as the roof of a house.'"
>
> —*The Broken Spears: The Aztec Account of the Conquest of Mexico*

_____ **18.** In this excerpt from an Aztec eyewitness, what is the "iron" being described?

   A. portable shelters
   B. wagons and supplies
   C. armor and weapons
   D. Spanish rowboats

_____ **19.** What are the tall "deer" that are mentioned in the passage?

   A. dogs   **C.** mastodons
   B. horses   **D.** wagons

_____ **20.** Refer to the passage. What is the messengers' attitude toward the Spaniards?

   A. The messengers are amused.
   B. The messengers are unimpressed.
   C. The messengers are terrified.
   D. The messengers are awestruck.

Chapter 1 Test, Traditional *cont.*

netw⊙rks

The First Americans

DIRECTIONS: Short Answer Answer each of the following questions.

Civilization	When	Where
Olmec	circa 1500 B.C. – 300 B.C.	present-day Mexico, Guatemala, Honduras
Maya	circa A.D. 300 – A.D. 1100	present-day Mexico, Guatemala, Honduras, Belize
Aztec	circa A.D. 1300 – A.D. 1521	present-day Mexico
Inca	circa A.D. 1200 – A.D. 1532	present-day Peru, Colombia, Argentina, Chile

21. Based on the chart, which present-day country was home to the greatest number of these early civilizations?

_____

22. Based on the chart, which civilization lasted the longest, and how long did it exist?

_____

23. Based on the chart, which civilization rose and fell the fastest, and how long did it exist?

_____

24. Based on the chart, which civilization ended most recently, and about how long ago did it end?

_____

DIRECTIONS: Essay Answer the following question on a separate piece of paper.

25. Choose three early Native American groups. Describe how each adapted to its environments.

Discovering Our Past: A History of the United States

Chapter 1 Test, Document-Based Questions

netw⦿rks

The First Americans

DIRECTIONS: Short Answer Answer each of the following questions.

> "A certain man had a Dog. One day the Dog looked westward and began howling. The man also had a hen and chickens which began to dance about in the stomp dance.
>
> "Then the man said to his Dog, 'Why are you howling?'
>
> "'I have discovered something that is making me howl. In about four days everything is going to be overflowed by water. You ought to make a raft on which to escape, gather all the wood you can on top of it, and keep a little fire burning upon it. When you have finished the raft plait a hickory rope with which to tie it so that it will not drift off into the ocean.'"
>
> —from *Myths and Tales of the Southeastern Indians*

1. In this excerpt from a Natchez myth, what two things first alert the man that something unusual is going on?

   _____

   _____

   _____

2. Which detail of this story would a reader today be least likely to fully understand, and why?

   _____

   _____

   _____

3. What tells today's reader that this story cannot be taken literally?

   _____

   _____

   _____

Chapter 1 Test, Document-Based Questions *cont.*

networks

The First Americans

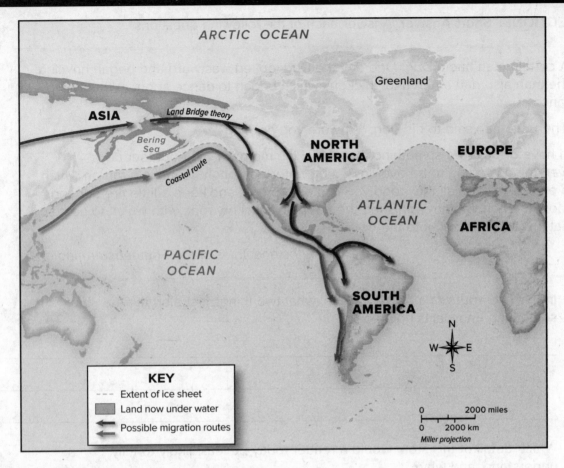

4. What would be a good title for this map?

_____

5. According to the map, what was the starting point for all prehistoric American migration?

_____

6. According to the map, in what general direction did early American migration flow?

_____

DIRECTIONS: Essay Answer the following question on a separate piece of paper.

7. Describe and explain the appearance of the first people in North and South America. State ways in which their cultures developed as they migrated.

Lesson Quiz 2-1

Exploring the Americas

DIRECTIONS: Completion Enter the appropriate word(s) to complete the statement.

1. The _____ helped make long sea voyages possible because it was both fast and large.

2. Religious expeditions called the _____ had the unplanned result of creating trade between Europe and Asia.

3. In the early A.D. 600s, a new religion called _____ began to spread quickly in the Middle East and Africa.

4. The French word *renaissance* means _____.

DIRECTIONS: Multiple Choice Indicate the answer choice that best completes the statement or answers the question.

_____ 5. Which of these is a navigational tool?

    A. an astrolabe

    B. a caravel

    C. a junk

    D. a crusade

_____ 6. Why did Portugal want to explore the world?

    A. to find new trade routes to Asia

    B. to test their technology

    C. to rule the world

    D. to satisfy their curiosity

_____ 7. After the fall of the Roman Empire, Western Europe was dominated by

    A. the New Roman Empire.

    B. the Catholic Church.

    C. China.

    D. the Renaissance.

_____ 8. Who painted the Mona Lisa?

    A. Marco Polo

    B. Leonardo Da Vinci

    C. Christopher Columbus

    D. the Almoravids

Lesson Quiz 2-2

networks

Exploring the Americas

DIRECTIONS: True/False Indicate whether the statement is true or false.

_____ **1.** By the time the period of European exploration began, most maps included the Americas.

_____ **2.** Vasco da Gama led voyages of exploration for Spain.

_____ **3.** The southern tip of Africa was renamed from the "Cape of Storms" to the "Cape of Good Hope" by Portugal's King John.

_____ **4.** Queen Isabella hoped to convert Native Americans to Christianity.

DIRECTIONS: Multiple Choice Indicate the answer choice that best answers the question.

_____ **5.** Which of these was the largest of the ships on Christopher Columbus's first voyage?

   A. the *Niña*

   B. the *Isabella*

   C. the *Santa María*

   D. the *Pinta*

_____ **6.** From where did Portuguese traders buy enslaved Africans in the mid-1400s?

   A. the Mediterranean Coast

   B. the Cape of Good Hope

   C. the Orange River

   D. the Gold Coast

_____ **7.** Who was the first explorer to realize that South America was not part of Asia?

   A. Christopher Columbus

   B. Vasco Núñez de Balboa

   C. Amerigo Vespucci

   D. Ferdinand Magellan

_____ **8.** Whose crew was the first to circumnavigate the world?

   A. Christopher Columbus

   B. Vasco Núñez de Balboa

   C. Amerigo Vespucci

   D. Ferdinand Magellan

Lesson Quiz 2-3

networks

Exploring the Americas

DIRECTIONS: Matching Match each item with its definition.

_____ **1.** Spanish explorer

_____ **2.** member of the Spanish upper class living in the Americas

_____ **3.** Spanish town in the Americas

_____ **4.** Spanish religious farming community

_____ **5.** Spanish fort

A. pueblo

B. conquistador

C. mission

D. peninsulare

E. presidio

DIRECTIONS: Multiple Choice Indicate the answer choice that best completes the statement or answers the question.

_____ **6.** Which of these powerful empires was conquered by Hernán Cortés?

    A. Aztec

    B. Inca

    C. Maya

    D. Seven Cities of Cíbola

_____ **7.** Whose army conquered the Inca Empire?

    A. Atahualpa

    B. Francisco Pizarro

    C. Hernán Cortés

    D. Montezuma

_____ **8.** Which of these was an essential part of the economy of the Spanish colonies?

    A. Native American currency

    B. priests

    C. enslaved workers

    D. tobacco

_____ **9.** After the arrival of Europeans, many Native Americans died because of

    A. disease.

    B. exposure to heat.

    C. overcrowded conditions.

    D. starvation.

Lesson Quiz 2-4

netw⚬rks

Exploring the Americas

DIRECTIONS: True/False Indicate whether the statement is true or false.

_____ **1.** Martin Luther started the Protestant Reformation by rejecting many teachings of the Catholic Church.

_____ **2.** Explorers searched the coast of North America looking for the Northwest Passage to Asia.

_____ **3.** The relationship between the French and the Native Americans in New France was unfriendly and threatened the way of life of the Native Americans.

DIRECTIONS: Multiple Choice Indicate the answer choice that best completes the statement or answers the question.

_____ **4.** The Reformation can best be described as

    A. a type of government.

    B. the study of scientific ideas.

    C. a religious movement.

    D. an artistic rebirth.

_____ **5.** What Italian explorer led expeditions for France?

    A. Giovanni da Verrazano

    B. Jacques Cartier

    C. Louis Joliet

    D. Samuel de Champlain

_____ **6.** Who searched for a passage through the Americas under the sponsorship of the Dutch?

    A. Christopher Columbus

    B. Henry Hudson

    C. John Cabot

    D. Robert de La Salle

_____ **7.** Which country's colonists maintained a profitable fur trade in North America?

    A. Denmark   **C.** France

    B. England   **D.** Spain

_____ **8.** The French established a royal colony that was named

    A. New France.   **C.** Marquette.

    B. Montreal.   **D.** New Amsterdam.

Chapter 2 Test, Traditional

netw⊙rks

Exploring the Americas

DIRECTIONS: True/False Indicate whether the statement is true or false.

_____ **1.** Portugal took the lead in finding a trade route to India.

_____ **2.** Information from explorers assisted mapmakers in creating more accurate land and sea maps.

_____ **3.** Beginning in the A.D. 600s, the religion of Islam spread in the Middle East and Africa.

_____ **4.** The Renaissance was the attempt by Europeans to take back control of Christian holy sites in the Middle East.

_____ **5.** Pizarro was able to conquer the Inca after the Spanish executed the Inca's ruler.

DIRECTIONS: Matching Match the explorer to the country for which he sailed. A country can be used more than once.

_____ **6.** Verrazano   **A.** France

_____ **7.** Cabot   **B.** Spain

_____ **8.** Cartier   **C.** England

_____ **9.** Columbus

_____ **10.** Cortés

Chapter 2 Test, Traditional *cont.*

Exploring the Americas

DIRECTIONS: Multiple Choice Indicate the answer choice that best completes the statement or answers the question.

_____ **11.** In 1492 Christopher Columbus sailed to America with the *Niña*, *Pinta*, and the

    A. *Cortés.*

    B. *Isabella.*

    C. *Santa María.*

    D. *Tordesillas.*

_____ **12.** Which conquistador landed on the east coast of present-day Mexico in 1519?

    A. Christopher Columbus

    B. Francisco Pizarro

    C. Hernán Cortés

    D. Juan Ponce de León

_____ **13.** What did England, France, and the Netherlands hope to discover in their explorations?

    A. a northwest passage to Asia

    B. a route to South America

    C. a route to Africa

    D. a southwest passage to India

_____ **14.** What did the French establish in the Americas?

    A. fishing and fur trade

    B. gold and silver mines

    C. new communities

    D. slave trade

_____ **15.** Which of these events was the first to take place?

    A. Magellan sails around the world.

    B. The first Crusade is launched.

    C. Marco Polo returns from China.

    D. Columbus sails to the Americas.

Discovering Our Past: A History of the United States

Exploring the Americas

> "Your Highnesses commanded me . . . [to] go to . . . India, and for this accorded me great rewards and ennobled [gave a title to] me so that from this time henceforth I might style myself 'Don' and be high admiral of the Ocean Sea and . . . Governor of the islands and continents which I should discover."
>
> —Christopher Columbus, in *The Journal of Christopher Columbus*

_____ **16.** In this excerpt, where does Columbus state he is being ordered to go?

  A. China

  B. India

  C. France

  D. San Salvador

_____ **17.** What reward awaited Columbus if his voyage was successful?

  A. owning a fleet of ships

  B. governing all discovered lands

  C. receiving great riches

  D. making a place in history

> "[The province of Quivira] is the best I have every seen for producing all the products of Spain . . . the land itself being very fat and black and being very well watered by the rivulets and spring and rivers, . . . I have treated the natives of this province, and all the others whom I found wherever I went, as well as possible, agreeable to what Your Majesty had commanded. . . . [T]here is not any gold nor any other metal in all that country, and the other things of which they had told me are nothing but little villages."
>
> —Francisco Vásquez de Coronado, letter to Charles I of Spain

_____ **18.** In this excerpt, what does Coronado report that he has discovered?

  A. some very rich land for farming

  B. the legendary "Seven Cities of Cíbola"

  C. native peoples to enslave

  D. vast silver and gold deposits

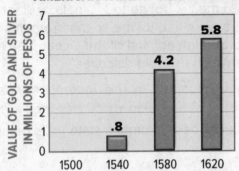

AMERICAN WEALTH SENT TO SPAIN

_____ **19.** According to this graph, how many more pesos' worth of gold and silver were sent to Spain from the Americas in 1620 than in 1540?

    A. 4 million   **C.** 5 million

    B. 4.8 million   **D.** 5.8 million

DIRECTIONS: Short Answer Answer each of the following questions.

20. Spanish law called for which three kinds of settlements in the Americas?

_____

21. What is the name given to an individual who paid rent and farmed for their lord for a set period each year?

_____

Spain: King Ferdinand and Queen Isabella	**Portugal:** King John II
• answered Columbus's plea for support	• rebuffed Columbus's plea for support
• sought a direct route to India not already controlled by Portugal	• already controlled some routes to India, including one along the African coast
• mainly interested in settlements, wealth, and spreading Christianity	• mainly interested in trade
• signed Treaty of Tordesillas that set bounds on each country's colonial expansion	• signed Treaty of Tordesillas that set bounds on each country's colonial expansion

22. According to the table, on how many points did the two countries agree?

_____

23. How did the interests of the countries differ?

_____

Chapter 2 Test, Document-Based Questions

netw⊙rks

Exploring the Americas

DIRECTIONS: Short Answer Answer each of the following questions on a separate piece of paper.

> "I have decided upon writing you this letter to acquaint you with all the events which have occurred in my voyage, and the discoveries which have resulted from it. Thirty-three days after my departure . . . I reached the Indian Sea, where I discovered many islands, thickly peopled, of which I took possession without resistance in the name of our most illustrious monarch, by public proclamation and with unfurled banners."
>
> — Letter from Christopher Columbus to Lord Raphael Sanchez, March 1493

1. When Columbus speaks of his "most illustrious monarch" in the passage above, to whom is he referring?

2. Columbus claimed the islands for Spain "by public proclamation and unfurled banners." To what does the phrase "unfurled banners" refer?

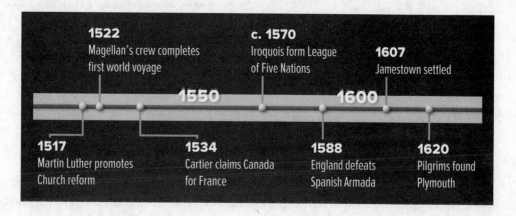

3. According to this time line, Magellan's crew completed their first voyage between which two events?

4. According to this time line, how many years passed between the settlement of Jamestown and the founding of Plymouth?

Discovering Our Past: A History of the United States

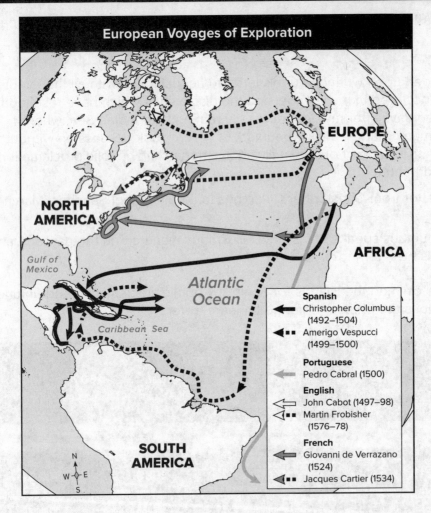

European Voyages of Exploration

5. Name the two explorers shown on the map above who sailed on behalf of France.

6. According to this map, which explorer traveled farthest west?

DIRECTIONS: Essay Answer the following question on a separate piece of paper.

> "Some [men] aim at gain, some at glory, some at the public weal [good]. The greater number are engaged in trade, and especially that which is transacted [done] on the sea. . . . This is what raised ancient Rome to the sovereignty and mastery over the entire world, and the Venetians to a grandeur [glory] equal to that of powerful kings. . . . For this reason, many princes have striven [tried] to find a northerly route to China, . . . in the belief that this route would be shorter and less dangerous."
>
> —Samuel de Champlain, *Voyages*, 1603

7. Champlain speaks of the importance of exploration in this quote. What are some of the reasons exploration was so important?

Lesson Quiz 3-1

networks

Colonial America

DIRECTIONS: Completion Enter the appropriate word(s) to complete the statement.

1. Although bad weather kept John White from investigating, he thought the Roanoke settlers might have moved to _____.

2. In a joint-stock company, investors buy shares, or part ownership, in the company in the hope of sharing future _____.

3. The men of Jamestown elected representatives called _____ to enact local laws.

4. When the Virginia Company sent _____ to Jamestown, marriage and children became part of life in Virginia.

5. In 1624 King James took control of the Virginia Colony from the Virginia Company, making the area a(n) _____ colony.

DIRECTIONS: Multiple Choice Indicate the answer choice that best completes the statement or answers the question.

_____ 6. What kept John White from returning to Roanoke for nearly three years?

    A. the collapse of the English economy

    B. the defeat of the Spanish Armada

    C. fighting between England and Spain

    D. his poor health

_____ 7. Which of the following is an example of a joint-stock company?

    A. the Drake Company   **C.** the Roanoke Company

    B. the England Company   **D.** the Virginia Company

_____ 8. The Jamestown colonists called the winter of 1609–1610

    A. the awful time.   **C.** the starving time.

    B. the feasting time.   **D.** the thoughtful time.

_____ 9. Which crop saved Jamestown by making money for the settlement's investors?

    A. corn   **C.** tobacco

    B. rice   **D.** wheat

_____ 10. The first English child born in the American colonies was

    A. Virginia Dare.   **C.** John White.

    B. Francis Drake.   **D.** James Yeardley.

Discovering Our Past: A History of the United States

Lesson Quiz 3-2

networks

Colonial America

DIRECTIONS: True/False Indicate whether the statement is true or false.

_____ **1.** The Pilgrims who came to America on the *Mayflower* were Puritans.

_____ **2.** The Pilgrims founded Jamestown.

_____ **3.** A group of Puritans led by John Winthrop established the Massachusetts Bay colony in 1630.

_____ **4.** A lack of religious tolerance by the Puritans led to the formation of colonies elsewhere.

_____ **5.** The outcome of King Philip's War enabled colonists to move into Native American territories.

DIRECTIONS: Multiple Choice Indicate the answer choice that best completes the statement or answers the question.

_____ **6.** Protestants who wanted to reform the Anglican Church were called

    A. Catholics.   **C.** Puritans.

    B. Protestant reformers.   **D.** Separatists.

_____ **7.** The Mayflower Compact was a

    A. pledge to obey the laws of the colony.

    B. promise to keep peace with Native Americans.

    C. pledge to the other colonies.

    D. religious loyalty contract.

_____ **8.** The Pilgrims survived in Plymouth due to the help of

    A. the Anglican Church.   **C.** King James II.

    B. Captain John Smith.   **D.** Squanto and Samoset.

_____ **9.** The first written constitution in America was the

    A. Fundamental Orders of Connecticut.

    B. Mayflower Compact.

    C. Plymouth Pledge.

    D. Virginia Compact.

_____ **10.** Where in America was religious tolerance first practiced?

    A. Boston   **C.** Plymouth

    B. Cape Cod   **D.** Rhode Island

Lesson Quiz 3-3

networks

Colonial America

DIRECTIONS: Matching Match each item with the correct statement below.

_____ 1. surrendered to the English without a fight in 1664

_____ 2. founded the colony of Pennsylvania

_____ 3. a landowner in New Netherland

_____ 4. someone who refuses to fight wars

_____ 5. the sole owner and ruler of a colony

A. Quakers

B. pacifist

C. patroon

D. Peter Stuyvesant

E. proprietor

DIRECTIONS: Multiple Choice Indicate the answer choice that best completes the statement or answers the question.

_____ 6. Which of these was originally called New Amsterdam?

    A. New Jersey   **C.** Philadelphia

    B. New York City   **D.** Rhode Island

_____ 7. Which of the following was named after an island in the English Channel?

    A. Delaware   **C.** New Jersey

    B. New Amsterdam   **D.** Pennsylvania

_____ 8. He designed the "City of Brotherly Love."

    A. Sir George Carteret

    B. Oliver Cromwell

    C. William Penn

    D. Peter Stuyvesant

_____ 9. What 1701 document granted Pennsylvania colonists the right to elect legislative representatives?

    A. the Charter of Colonists

    B. the Charter of Pennsylvania

    C. the Charter of Privileges

    D. Penn's Charter

_____ 10. William Penn allowed some of Pennsylvania's southern counties to function as a separate colony called

    A. Delaware.   **C.** Philadelphia.

    B. New Amsterdam.   **D.** New Pennsylvania.

Lesson Quiz 3-4

network

Colonial America

DIRECTIONS: Completion Enter the appropriate word(s) to complete the statement.

1. _____ servants were settlers who paid for their passage to America by working without pay for a period of time.

2. Bacon's Rebellion was a revolt against the government of the _____ colony.

3. People from the continent of _____ were enslaved in the Southern Colonies.

4. In 1676 Nathaniel Bacon led a series of attacks against villages inhabited by _____.

5. Founded in 1733, _____ was the last English colony established in North America.

DIRECTIONS: Multiple Choice Indicate the answer choice that best completes the statement or answers the question.

_____ 6. Which colony was founded as a place for Catholics to practice their religion freely?

    A. Georgia

    B. Maryland

    C. North Carolina

    D. South Carolina

_____ 7. Which of these Carolina crops was developed in the 1740s by Eliza Lucas?

    A. corn   **C.** lumber

    B. indigo   **D.** rice

_____ 8. Which of these colonies was established as a place for debtors to make a fresh start?

    A. Georgia   **C.** North Carolina

    B. Maryland   **D.** South Carolina

_____ 9. The word "Carolina" is Latin for

    A. "Charles's Land."

    B. "King's Land."

    C. "North of Georgia."

    D. "Penn's Land."

Chapter 3 Test, Traditional

networks

Colonial America

DIRECTIONS: True/False Indicate whether the statement is true or false.

_____ **1.** By 1750, Dutch colonies stretched for hundreds of miles along the Atlantic coast.

_____ **2.** The settlers of Roanoke vanished around 1590, never to be seen again.

_____ **3.** The Pilgrims first dropped anchor in Cape Cod Bay.

_____ **4.** The word "Pennsylvania" means "Penn's experiment."

_____ **5.** A constitution is a list of a government's fundamental laws.

DIRECTIONS: Matching Match each item with the correct statement below.

_____ **6.** one of New Jersey's proprietors

_____ **7.** Pilgrim colony

_____ **8.** Jamestown's legislative assembly

_____ **9.** founder of Hartford, Connecticut

_____ **10.** Virginia's governor

A. House of Burgesses

B. Lord John Berkeley

C. Plymouth

D. Thomas Hooker

E. William Berkeley

DIRECTIONS: Multiple Choice Indicate the answer choice that best completes the statement or answers the question.

_____ **11.** The Jamestown settlers made a profit for their investors by raising

A. cotton.

B. maize.

C. tobacco.

D. wheat.

_____ **12.** What did groups of merchants obtain from the British king in order to start settlements in America?

A. compacts

B. charters

C. pledges

D. stocks

_____ **13.** Protestants who left the Anglican Church and established their own churches were called

A. Anglicans.

B. New Anglicans.

C. Puritans.

D. Separatists.

_____ **14.** The Massachusetts Bay Company was granted a charter to establish a colony north of

    A. Boston.

    B. Mayflower.

    C. Plymouth.

    D. Rhode Island.

_____ **15.** Pacifists are people who

    A. refuse to fight in wars.

    B. sail in the Pacific Ocean.

    C. serve in government office.

    D. explore new territories.

Founding the Thirteen Colonies			
Colony	**First Permanent Settlement**	**Reasons Founded**	**Founders or Leaders**
New England Colonies			
Massachusetts Plymouth Mass. Bay Colony	1620 1630	Religious freedom Religious freedom	John Carver, William Bradford John Winthrop
New Hampshire	c. 1620	Profit from trade and fishing	Ferdinando Gorges, John Mason
Rhode Island	1636	Religious freedom	Roger Williams
Connecticut	1636	Profit from fur trade, farming, religious and political freedom	Thomas Hooker
Middle Colonies			
New York	1624	Expand trade	Dutch settlers
Delaware	1638	Expand trade	Swedish settlers
New Jersey	1638	Profit from selling land	John Berkeley, George Carteret
Pennsylvania	1682	Profit from selling land; religious freedom	William Penn

Table continued on next page

Discovering Our Past: A History of the United States

Chapter 3 Test, Traditional *cont.*

netw⊙rks

Colonial America

Founding the Thirteen Colonies			
Southern Colonies			
Virginia	1607	Expand trade	John Smith
Maryland	1634	To sell land; religious freedom	Cecil Calvert
North Carolina	c. 1660s	Profit from trade and selling land	Group of eight aristocrats
South Carolina	1670	Profit from trade and selling land	Group of eight aristocrats
Georgia	1735	Religious freedom; protection against Spanish Florida; safe home for debtors	James Oglethorpe

_____ **16.** According to the chart, which was the last of the thirteen colonies to be settled?

    A. Georgia   **C.** Pennsylvania

    B. Massachusetts   **D.** Virginia

_____ **17.** According to the chart, why were the New York and Virginia colonies founded?

    A. for religious freedom   **C.** to profit from fishing

    B. to expand trade   **D.** to profit from selling land

_____ **18.** According to the chart, how many colonies were founded for the purpose of religious freedom?

    A. 2   **C.** 9

    B. 7   **D.** 13

DIRECTIONS: Short Answer Answer each of the following questions.

19. According to the chart, which of the Southern Colonies were founded for religious freedom?

_____

20. According to the chart, how many colonies were founded with the purpose of making a profit?

_____

Chapter 3 Test, Traditional *cont.*

networks

Colonial America

21. What does the name "Pocahontas" mean?

_____

22. What sort of political principles guided the creation of the Fundamental Orders of Connecticut and the Mayflower Compact?

_____

_____

_____

DIRECTIONS: Essay Answer the following question.

23. Why do you think some people in England objected to the Quakers and persecuted them?

_____

_____

_____

_____

_____

_____

_____

_____

Discovering Our Past: A History of the United States

Chapter 3 Test, Document-Based Questions

netw⊙rks

Colonial America

DIRECTIONS: Short Answer Answer each of the following questions.

"[Our overseer] gave the same task to each slave; of course the weak ones often failed to do it. I have often seen him tie up persons and flog them in the morning, only because they were unable to get the previous day's task done: after they were flogged, pork or beef brine was put on their bleeding backs, to increase the pain; he sitting by resting himself, and seeing it done. After being thus flogged and pickled, the sufferers often remained tied up all day, the feet just touching the ground, the legs tied, and pieces of wood put between the legs. All the motion allowed was a slight turn of the neck. Thus exposed and helpless, the yellow flies and mosquitoes in great numbers would settle on the bleeding and smarting back, and put the sufferer to extreme torture. This continued all day, for they were not taken down till night."

—Moses Grandy, *Life of a Slave* (1843)

1. This account is by a formerly enslaved person who worked on a Southern plantation before the Civil War. How did the overseer treat the enslaved people?

   _____

   _____

   _____

2. Overseers were people who supervised enslaved people. Why do you think overseers were used?

   _____

   _____

   _____

3. How would you describe the emotion that Grandy expresses in this excerpt?

   _____

   _____

   _____

Enslaved People in the Colonies			
Year	North	South	Total
1650	880	720	1,600
1670	1,125	3,410	4,535
1690	3,340	13,389	16,729
1710	8,303	36,563	44,866

4. According to the chart, when did the North's enslaved population grow the most?

_____

5. According to the chart, when did the South's enslaved population grow the most?

_____

6. From about 1670 on, which area had the largest population of enslaved people?

_____

DIRECTIONS: Essay Answer the following question on a separate piece of paper.

7. Why and where did slavery arise and grow in the American Colonies?

Lesson Quiz 4-1

netw⊙rks

Life in the American Colonies

DIRECTIONS: Matching Match each item with its definition.

_____ 1. important New England industry

_____ 2. rules created to control enslaved people

_____ 3. crops that sold easily

_____ 4. cultural variety

_____ 5. near Appalachian Mountains

A. cash crops

B. backcountry

C. slave codes

D. shipbuilding

E. diversity

DIRECTIONS: Multiple Choice Indicate the answer choice that best completes the statement or answers the question.

_____ 6. Which of the following means producing just enough to meet the family's needs, with little left over to sell or exchange?

    A. harvesting

    B. cash cropping

    C. subsistence farming

    D. tidewater farming

_____ 7. The most inhumane aspect of the triangular trade was the

    A. fishing trade.

    B. merchant trade route.

    C. Middle Passage.

    D. Southern Route.

_____ 8. Where were most of the large Southern plantations located?

    A. backcountry

    B. coastal areas

    C. flatlands

    D. Tidewater

_____ 9. The plantation bosses who kept the enslaved Africans working hard were called

    A. employers.

    B. overseers.

    C. slaveholders.

    D. supervisors.

_____ 10. Which group controlled the economic and political life of the Southern Colonies?

    A. farmers

    B. merchants

    C. plantation owners

    D. teachers

Lesson Quiz 4-2

networks

Life in the American Colonies

DIRECTIONS: True/False Indicate whether the statement is true or false.

_____ **1.** During the Glorious Revolution, the British monarchy gained more power at the expense of Parliament.

_____ **2.** After the Navigation Acts were passed, colonial merchants could not use foreign ships to send their goods.

_____ **3.** King James II succeeded William and Mary in a peaceful transfer of power.

_____ **4.** The colonists resisted the Navigation Acts because they wanted to manufacture their own goods.

_____ **5.** The idea of representative government was introduced by the colonists.

DIRECTIONS: Matching Match each item with the correct statement below.

_____ **6.** economic theory

_____ **7.** trading illegally

_____ **8.** royal colonies

_____ **9.** peaceful transfer of power in England

_____ **10.** proprietary colonies

A. ruled by Britain

B. Glorious Revolution

C. smuggling

D. ruled as owners wished

E. mercantilism

Discovering Our Past: A History of the United States

Lesson Quiz 4-3

networks

Life in the American Colonies

DIRECTIONS: Multiple Choice Indicate the answer choice that best completes the statement or answers the question.

_____ 1. The main reason for population growth in the colonies was

    A. epidemics.   **C.** immigration.

    B. health care.   **D.** large families.

_____ 2. What were the first colleges set up to do in the colonies?

    A. to train craftspeople   **C.** to train ministers

    B. to train doctors   **D.** to train women

_____ 3. The American who best exemplified the Enlightenment way of thinking was

    A. Jonathan Edwards.   **C.** William Penn.

    B. Benjamin Franklin.   **D.** George Whitefield.

_____ 4. Although widows and unmarried women enjoyed certain rights, they could not

    A. work outside the home.

    B. own property.

    C. vote.

    D. run businesses.

_____ 5. The Great Awakening represented

    A. a renewed interest in science.

    B. a religious revival.

    C. new ideas about freedom.

    D. a renewed belief in civic virtue.

DIRECTIONS: Short Answer Answer each of the following questions on a separate piece of paper.

6. What were three things that contributed to American culture?

7. Which case was an important step toward the idea of freedom of the press?

8. How did most children learn to read and write?

9. What were some of the roles for married women in the colonies?

10. What is civic virtue?

Lesson Quiz 4-4

netw⊙rks

Life in the American Colonies

DIRECTIONS: Multiple Choice Indicate the answer choice that best completes the statement or answers the question.

_____ 1. What was the name of the small post that George Washington established in Ohio country?

    A. Fort Albany Union   **C.** Fort Monongahela

    B. Fort Duquesne   **D.** Fort Necessity

_____ 2. By 1700, the major powers in North America were the

    A. British and French.   **C.** French and Spanish.

    B. British and Spanish.   **D.** French and Dutch.

_____ 3. During the wars between France and Great Britain, Native Americans often helped the French by

    A. raiding British settlements.   **C.** supplying their weapons.

    B. showing them secret paths.   **D.** supplying them with food.

_____ 4. The British prime minister who drove the French out of America was

    A. Edward Braddock.   **C.** William Pitt.

    B. Benjamin Franklin.   **D.** George Washington.

_____ 5. What document marked the end of France as a power in North America?

    A. Treaty of France and Britain

    B. Treaty of the Ohio River Valley

    C. Adams–Onís Treaty

    D. Treaty of Paris

DIRECTIONS: Short Answer Answer each of the following questions on a separate piece of paper.

  6. Which nations made up the Iroquois Confederacy?

  7. Why did the Albany Plan of Union fail?

  8. Why were the French and the Native Americans allies?

  9. What was Pitt's plan in regard to how to deal with the cost of the French and Indian War?

 10. How did the French defeat affect Native Americans in the Ohio River Valley?

Chapter 4 Test, Traditional

networks

Life in the American Colonies

DIRECTIONS: True/False Indicate whether the statement is true or false.

_____ 1. Most colonists placed a high value on education.

_____ 2. The Enlightenment was a religious movement.

_____ 3. The case involving John Peter Zenger was an important step in establishing freedom of the press in America.

_____ 4. One of William Pitt's goals for the French and Indian War was to conquer French Canada.

_____ 5. The Proclamation of 1763 ended the French and Indian War.

DIRECTIONS: Matching Match each item with the correct statement below.

_____ 6. partnership of two parties

_____ 7. powerful group of Native Americans

_____ 8. author of Albany Plan of Union

_____ 9. to change the religious beliefs of someone

_____ 10. increased interest in science

A. Iroquois Confederacy

B. convert

C. Benjamin Franklin

D. alliance

E. Enlightenment

DIRECTIONS: Multiple Choice Indicate the answer choice that best completes the statement or answers the question.

_____ 11. Which of the following directed the flow of goods between England and the colonies?

    A. Colonies' Charter   **C.** Merchant's Pledge

    B. Colonists Rights Law   **D.** Navigation Acts

_____ 12. A colony in which an owner or a group of owners named the colony's governor is called a

    A. charter colony.   **C.** proprietary colony.

    B. compact colony.   **D.** royal colony.

_____ 13. Who were the only people who could vote in the colonies?

    A. indentured servants   **C.** white female property owners

    B. landless white men   **D.** white male property owners

_____ **14.** Where was George Washington's first command?

    A. Appalachian Mountains

    B. Blue Ridge Mountains

    C. Ohio River Valley

    D. Virginia territory

_____ **15.** The Proclamation of 1763 called for

    A. a halt to westward expansion.

    B. a war.

    C. Native Americans to move west.

    D. settlers to move westward.

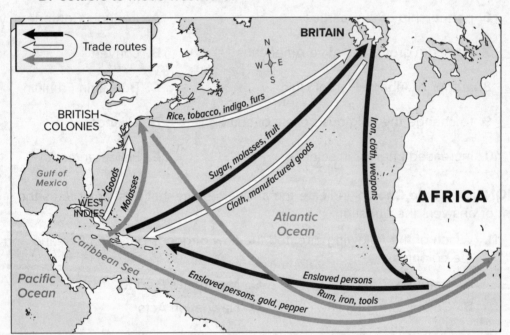

_____ **16.** Based on the map, what besides enslaved people was imported to the New World from Africa?

    A. gold, pepper   **C.** iron, tools

    B. indigo, furs   **D.** rice, tobacco

_____ **17.** What would be the best title for the map?

    A. European Settlement Patterns

    B. Great Awakening

    C. National Origins of Colonists

    D. Triangular Trade Routes

Chapter 4 Test, Traditional *cont.*

Life in the American Colonies

_____ **18.** Some people in New England used waterpower from streams to

    A. make electricity for their homes.

    B. power manufacturing plants.

    C. power plows and other farm equipment.

    D. run grain and lumber mills.

_____ **19.** What was the main cash crop of South Carolina and Georgia?

    A. cotton   **C.** tobacco

    B. rice   **D.** wheat

DIRECTIONS: Short Answer Answer each of the following questions.

> "Viewed and considered as a settlement, Virginia is far from being arrived at that degree of perfection which it is capable of. Not a tenth of the land is yet cultivated: and that which is cultivated, is far from being so in the most advantageous manner. It produces, however, considerable quantities of grain and cattle, and fruit of many kinds. The Virginian pork is said to be superior in flavour to any in the world, but the sheep and horned cattle being small and lean, the meat of them is inferior to that of Great Britain, or indeed, of most parts of Europe. The horses are fleet and beautiful; and the gentlemen of Virginia, who are exceedingly fond of horse-racing, have spared no expence or trouble to improve the breed."
>
> —Andrew Burnaby, 1775

20. What is this young English traveler's opinion of what he finds in Virginia?

_____

_____

_____

_____

_____

_____

Chapter 4 Test, Traditional *cont.*

networks

21. What were the two largest cities in the colonies?

_____

22. What were some of the restrictions of the slave codes?

_____

_____

_____

_____

African Slave Trade, 1450–1870	
Destination	**Total**
British America/United States	427,000
Mexico and Central America	224,000
West Indies	4,040,000
Spanish South America	522,000
Guianas	531,000
Brazil	3,647,000
Europe	175,000

23. From the information provided in the chart, which location received the most enslaved people during the period 1450–1870?

_____

DIRECTIONS: Essay Answer the following question on a separate piece of paper.

24. Why were the Native Americans so important in the clash between the French and British? Who had the advantage with the Native Americans and why?

Chapter 4 Test, Document-Based Questions

networks

Life in the American Colonies

DIRECTIONS: Short Answer Answer each of the following questions on a separate piece of paper.

> "The Petition of a Grate Number of Blackes of this Province who by divine permission are held in a state of Slavery within the bowels of a free and christian Country
>
> "Humbly Shewing
>
> "That your Petitioners apprehind we have in common with all other men a naturel right to our freedoms without Being depriv'd of them by our fellow men as we are a freeborn Pepel and have never forfeited this Blessing by aney compact or agreement whatever. But we were unjustly dragged by the cruel hand of power from our dearest frinds and sum of us stolen from the bosoms of our tender Parents and from a Populous Pleasant and plentiful country and Brought hither to be made slaves for Life in a Christian land. Thus we are deprived of every thing that hath a tendency to make life even tolerable, the endearing ties of husband and wife we are strangers to for we are no longer man and wife then our masters or mestreses thinkes proper marred or onmarred. Our children are also taken from us by force and sent maney miles from us wear we seldom or ever see them again there to be made slaves of for Life which sumtimes is vere short by Reson of Being dragged from their mothers Breest Thus our Lives are imbittered to us on these accounts."
>
> —"Slave Petition to the Governor, Council, and House of Representatives of the Province of Massachusetts," 1774

1. Why does this group of enslaved people in Massachusetts say that they should be free?

2. What did the enslaved people lose in addition to their freedom?

3. What do the writers say they have in common with other people?

CAUSES AND EFFECTS OF THE SLAVE TRADE

CAUSES

- Colonists need to grow cash crops, such as tobacco and rice.
- European demand for tobacco and rice increases.
- Growing tobacco and rice requires large labor force.

EFFECTS

- Africans are robbed of basic human rights.
- Population of enslaved Africans grows.
- Slavery creates feelings of injustice and plants seeds of regional conflict.

4. Based on this chart, what was the main motivation for the colonists to enter the slave trade?

5. Which important value did the colonists set aside when they participated in the slave trade?

DIRECTIONS: Essay Answer the following question on a separate piece of paper.

6. Compare and contrast the experience of the colonists and the enslaved who came to the New World.

Lesson Quiz 5-1

networks

The Spirit of Independence

DIRECTIONS: Completion Enter the appropriate word(s) to complete the statement.

1. Great Britain developed a huge debt from fighting the _____.

2. Officers could seize goods from accused smugglers without going to _____ as a result of the Sugar Act.

3. Angered by the _____, colonists believed they should be taxed only by their own assemblies.

4. The Sons of Liberty organized protests and burned _____ of tax collectors.

5. One of the ways women protested the Townshend Acts was by _____.

DIRECTIONS: Multiple Choice Indicate the answer choice that best completes the statement or answers the question.

_____ 6. What did writs of assistance allow British customs officers to search?

    A. foreigners   **C.** homes for smuggled goods

    B. foreign goods   **D.** people for contraband

_____ 7. Which of the following allowed the colonists to pay lower taxes on molasses?

    A. Proclamation of 1763   **C.** Sugar Act

    B. Stamp Act   **D.** writ of assistance

_____ 8. Which act taxed colonists without their consent?

    A. Declaratory Act   **C.** Sugar Act

    B. Stamp Act   **D.** Townshend Acts

_____ 9. Goods being imported to the colonies were taxed by which act?

    A. Declaratory Act   **C.** Sugar Act

    B. Stamp Act   **D.** Townshend Acts

_____ 10. Which act stated that Parliament did have the right to tax colonists?

    A. Declaratory Act   **C.** Sugar Act

    B. Stamp Act   **D.** Townshend Acts

Lesson Quiz 5-2

networks

The Spirit of Independence

DIRECTIONS: True/False Indicate whether the statement is true or false.

_____ **1.** Twenty colonists were killed during the Boston Massacre.

_____ **2.** Boycotts following the Boston Massacre helped repeal the Townshend Acts.

_____ **3.** The committee of correspondence was a system of letter writing between the colonial governors and the king.

_____ **4.** At the time of the Boston Tea Party, most colonists still considered themselves British citizens.

_____ **5.** Parliament successfully isolated Boston from the rest of the colonies by passing the Coercive Acts.

DIRECTIONS: Multiple Choice Indicate the answer choice that best completes the statement or answers the question.

_____ **6.** When Britain learned that the colonies were on the brink of rebellion in 1768, what was Parliament's response?

  A. Parliament closed Boston Harbor.

  B. Parliament did nothing.

  C. Parliament sent a letter to the colonies.

  D. Parliament sent troops to Boston.

_____ **7.** Paul Revere's engraving of which event was an example of propaganda that led to more intense anti-British feelings among the colonists?

  A. Boston Massacre   **C.** Intolerable Acts

  B. Boston Tea Party   **D.** *Liberty* Affair

_____ **8.** Which act gave the East India Company an advantage over colonial merchants?

  A. Declaratory Act   **C.** Sugar Act

  B. Stamp Act   **D.** Tea Act

_____ **9.** What was the dramatic act of defiance that some colonists celebrated?

  A. Boston Massacre   **C.** Coercive Acts

  B. Boston Tea Party   **D.** Intolerable Acts

Lesson Quiz 5-3

networks

The Spirit of Independence

DIRECTIONS: Matching Match each item with the correct statement below.

_____ **1.** voted to boycott British trade

_____ **2.** storage place for arms

_____ **3.** sold military information to the British

_____ **4.** warned that the British were coming

_____ **5.** leader of minutemen

A. Paul Revere

B. Continental Congress

C. Concord

D. Captain John Parker

E. Benedict Arnold

DIRECTIONS: Multiple Choice Indicate the answer choice that best completes the statement or answers the question.

_____ **6.** Who said that "blows must decide" who would rule America?

A. Edward III
B. George III
C. James III
D. Philip III

_____ **7.** Who had orders to take away the weapons of the Massachusetts militia?

A. George Washington
B. Paul Revere
C. Thomas Gage
D. William Dawes

_____ **8.** Who, along with Paul Revere, warned Samuel Adams that the British were coming?

A. George Washington
B. John Adams
C. Thomas Gage
D. William Dawes

_____ **9.** Who led the Green Mountain Boys who captured the British-held Fort Ticonderoga?

A. Ethan Allen
B. George Washington
C. Paul Revere
D. Ralph Waldo Emerson

_____ **10.** After winning which battle did the British learn that defeating the Americans would not be easy?

A. Battle of Boston
B. Battle of Bunker Hill
C. Battle of Concord
D. Battle of Lexington

Lesson Quiz 5-4

networks

The Spirit of Independence

DIRECTIONS: True/False Indicate whether the statement is true or false.

_____ 1. The Second Continental Congress established a post office with Benjamin Franklin in charge.

_____ 2. The king of Great Britain accepted the Olive Branch Petition offered by Congress.

_____ 3. The king hired German troops to fight in America.

_____ 4. Washington and his troops drove the British from New York in March 1776.

_____ 5. The Declaration of Independence explains why the colonies chose to form a new nation.

DIRECTIONS: Multiple Choice Indicate the answer choice that best completes the statement or answers the question.

_____ 6. Which group did the colonies organize to fight against Great Britain?

   A. Colonial Army   **C.** Continental Congress

   B. Continental Army   **D.** Redcoat Army

_____ 7. Who was the first commander of the Continental Army?

   A. Benjamin Franklin   **C.** John Adams

   B. George Washington   **D.** Thomas Jefferson

_____ 8. What did the Olive Branch Petition ask the king to do?

   A. leave America

   B. protect the colonists' rights

   C. go to war against France

   D. stop taxation

_____ 9. Who led the failed American attack on Quebec?

   A. Benedict Arnold   **C.** John Hancock

   B. George Washington   **D.** William Howe

_____ 10. Who was the first man to sign the Declaration of Independence?

   A. Benjamin Franklin   **C.** John Hancock

   B. John Adams   **D.** Thomas Jefferson

Discovering Our Past: A History of the United States

Chapter 5 Test, Traditional

networks

The Spirit of Independence

DIRECTIONS: True/False Indicate whether the statement is true or false.

_____ **1.** The Proclamation of 1763 helped Britain control westward expansion.

_____ **2.** The Stamp Act outraged colonists because they believed only Parliament could tax them.

_____ **3.** One of the Coercive Acts forced the colonies to allow British soldiers to live among the colonists.

_____ **4.** Some colonists were Loyalists who sided with Britain; the other colonists were Patriots who supported the right to independence.

_____ **5.** The Second Continental Congress chose Thomas Jefferson to command the Continental Army.

DIRECTIONS: Matching Match each item with the correct statement below.

_____ **6.** victim of Boston Massacre

_____ **7.** wrote a pamphlet calling for a break with British rule

_____ **8.** president of Second Continental Congress

_____ **9.** leader of the Green Mountain Boys

_____ **10.** organized the Sons of Liberty

A. Thomas Paine

B. Samuel Adams

C. Ethan Allen

D. Crispus Attucks

E. John Hancock

DIRECTIONS: Multiple Choice Indicate the answer choice that best completes the statement or answers the question.

_____ **11.** What did some colonists do to avoid taxes?

    A. They argued for more taxes.

    B. They moved to the Atlantic Coast.

    C. They resorted to smuggling.

    D. They went to court.

_____ **12.** Why were colonists angry after the Tea Act?

    A. They wanted Parliament to remove some of the taxes on tea.

    B. They wanted the ships to deliver tea to Boston Harbor.

    C. They wanted to make their own decisions about what tea to buy.

    D. They wanted to purchase East India Company tea.

_____ **13.** What was the political body that represented Americans and challenged British control?

    A. Coercive Acts   **C.** Sons of Liberty

    B. Continental Congress   **D.** Suffolk Resolves

_____ **14.** How did Parliament react to the news of the Boston Tea Party?

    A. Parliament decided to boycott tea.

    B. Parliament passed the Coercive Acts.

    C. Parliament sent food and clothing to Boston.

    D. Parliament tried to hold meetings in Boston.

_____ **15.** What was Thomas Paine's opinion about the colonies and Great Britain?

    A. The colonies should break from British rule.

    B. The colonies should continue to be taxed by Britain.

    C. The colonies should remain under British rule.

    D. The colonies should stop fighting the British.

_____ **16.** Where did many colonists believe fighting with the British would first break out?

    A. Great Britain   **C.** Philadelphia

    B. New England   **D.** Virginia

_____ **17.** Thomas Jefferson drew on the ideas of which English philosopher when writing the Declaration of Independence?

    A. George Mason   **C.** John Adams

    B. George Stout   **D.** John Locke

Chapter 5 Test, Traditional *cont.*

netw⊙rks

The Spirit of Independence

> "The battle, sir, is not to the strong alone; it is to the vigilant, the active, the brave. . . .
> If we were base enough to desire it, it is now too late to retire from the contest.
> There is no retreat but in submission and slavery! Our chains are forged! Their
> clanking may be heard on the plains of Boston! The war is inevitable—and let it
> come! I repeat it, sir, let it come.
>
> ". . . Gentlemen may cry Peace, Peace—but there is no peace. The war is actually
> begun!
>
> ". . . Our brethren are already in the field! Why stand we here idle? What is it that
> gentlemen wish? . . . Is life so dear, or peace so sweet, as to be purchased at the
> price of chains and slavery? Forbid it, Almighty God! I know not what course others
> may take; but as for me, give me liberty, or give me death!"
>
> —Patrick Henry, Speech to the Second Virginia Convention, 1775

_____ 18. What does Patrick Henry declare in this speech?

    A. An appeal to the British Parliament is necessary.

    B. Liberty cannot be won by fighting.

    C. The American colonies should be careful.

    D. War is unavoidable and he welcomes it.

_____ 19. Based on Patrick Henry's words, which side does he favor?

    A. the Independents

    B. the Loyalists

    C. the Parliament

    D. the Patriots

Chapter 5 Test, Traditional *cont.*

networks

The Spirit of Independence

DIRECTIONS: Short Answer Answer each of the following questions.

Taxes: One of the Causes of the Colonial Unrest

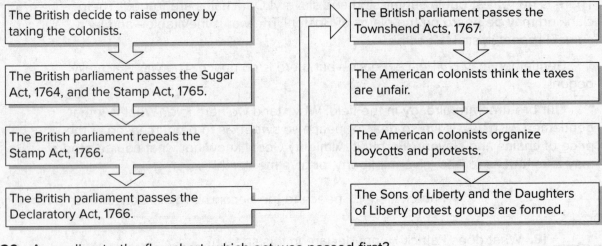

20. According to the flowchart, which act was passed first?

_____

21. According to the flowchart, during which years were these acts passed?

_____

22. What were some of the things that encouraged the Boston Massacre?

_____

_____

23. Why were some militias known as minutemen?

_____

DIRECTIONS: Essay Answer the following question on a separate piece of paper.

24. Distinguish between the First Continental Congress and the Second Continental Congress by discussing the decisions of each.

Chapter 5 Test, Document-Based Questions

networks

The Spirit of Independence

DIRECTIONS: Short Answer Answer each of the following questions on a separate piece of paper.

Taxes: One of the Causes of the Colonial Unrest

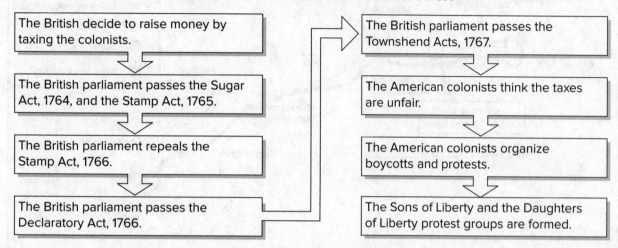

1. According to the flowchart, why did the British pass the Sugar Act and the Stamp Act?

2. According to the flowchart, why were the colonists so angry over these taxes?

"This new World hath been the asylum for the persecuted lovers of civil and religious liberty from EVERY PART of Europe. Hither have they fled, not from the tender embraces of the mother, but from the cruelty of the monster; and it is so far true of England, that the same tyranny which drove the first emigrants from home, pursues their descendants still. . . . 'A government of our own is our natural right. . . . 'O ye that love mankind! Ye that dare oppose not only the tyranny, but the tyrant, stand forth! Every spot of the old world is overrun with oppression. Freedom hath been hunted round the globe. . . . Europe regards her like a stranger, and England hath given her warning to depart. O! receive the fugitive, and prepare in time an asylum for mankind."

—Thomas Paine, *Common Sense*, 1776

3. Based on his writing, how does Thomas Paine view the Americas' role for humankind?

4. Based on his writing in *Common Sense*, was Thomas Paine a Loyalist or a Patriot?

Chapter 5 Test, Document-Based
Questions *cont.*

netw⚙rks

The Spirit of Independence

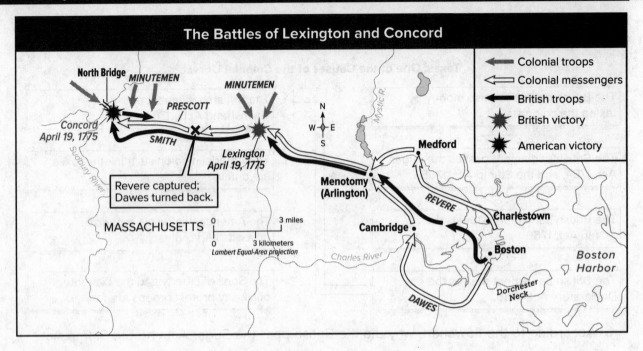

The Battles of Lexington and Concord

5. According to the map, which city was the starting point for British troops?

6. According to the map, what happened to British troops at Concord?

DIRECTIONS: Essay Answer the following question on a separate piece of paper.

7. After the French and Indian War, a conflict between American colonies and the British government developed. Why did this happen? In your answer include examples of the British policies and colonists' reactions. Also, include details about what motivated the colonists to fight and declare independence.

Lesson Quiz 6-1

networks

The American Revolution

DIRECTIONS: True/False Indicate whether the statement is true or false.

_____ **1.** The colonists had a large, well-trained army compared to the British.

_____ **2.** Hessians were hired German soldiers who fought for the colonists.

_____ **3.** In the early years of the war, the size of the Continental Army dwindled largely because soldiers left as their year of service was completed.

_____ **4.** Washington and his troops crossed the Delaware River and drove the enemy from Philadelphia.

_____ **5.** The American victory at Saratoga stopped the British plan to separate New England from the rest of the colonies.

DIRECTIONS: Multiple Choice Indicate the answer choice that best completes the statement or answers the question.

_____ **6.** Who disguised herself as a man so she could fight with the army?

    A. Margaret Corbin   **C.** Betsy Ross

    B. Molly Pitcher   **D.** Deborah Sampson

_____ **7.** Few patriots believed _____ when he stated, "We shall have a long . . . and bloody war to go through."

    A. John Adams   **C.** Thomas Paine

    B. Alexander Hamilton   **D.** George Washington

_____ **8.** The first state to have an all-African American regiment was

    A. Georgia.   **C.** Rhode Island.

    B. New York.   **D.** South Carolina.

_____ **9.** On October 17, 1777, General John Burgoyne surrendered to the Americans at

    A. Concord.   **C.** Saratoga.

    B. Philadelphia.   **D.** Trenton.

_____ **10.** In general, Loyalist support for Britain was weakest in

    A. Georgia.   **C.** North Carolina.

    B. New England.   **D.** Pennsylvania.

Lesson Quiz 6-2

netw⊕rks

The American Revolution

DIRECTIONS: Completion Enter the appropriate word(s) to complete the statement.

1. France realized that the United States might win the war after the American victory at
   _____.

2. When Lafayette arrived in Philadelphia from France, he offered his services to
   _____.

3. Juan de Miralles was largely responsible for Spain, Cuba, and Mexico sending
   _____ to help the colonies.

4. Financing the war was a problem for the Americans because the Continental Congress
   had no power to raise money through _____.

5. The ideals of freedom and liberty caused some Americans to question the institution of
   _____.

DIRECTIONS: Multiple Choice Indicate the answer choice that best completes the statement or answers the question.

_____ 6. George Washington's greatest challenge at Valley Forge was keeping

      A. the British away.   **C.** his army together.

      B. his spirits up.   **D.** entertainment for his army.

_____ 7. Which problem caused Congress to stop issuing paper money?

      A. winter weather   **C.** slavery

      B. inflation   **D.** poor soldier morale

_____ 8. The man who turned the ragged Continental Army into a more efficient fighting force was

      A. Casimir Pulaski.   **C.** Juan de Miralles.

      B. Thaddeus Kosciuszko.   **D.** Friedrich von Steuben.

_____ 9. The nation that made an alliance with the revolutionary United States in 1778 was

      A. Canada.   **C.** Great Britain.

      B. France.   **D.** Spain.

Lesson Quiz 6-3

netw⊙rks

The American Revolution

DIRECTIONS: True/False Indicate whether the statement is true or false.

_____ 1. More Native Americans fought on the side of the British than with the Americans during the American Revolution.

_____ 2. The 13 American warships that the Continental Congress ordered to be built made the American navy a powerful and effective force.

_____ 3. The British decided to concentrate their efforts in the South partly because the South had many Loyalists.

_____ 4. The British captured both Savannah, Georgia, and Charles Town, South Carolina.

_____ 5. After realizing that he could not control North Carolina, Cornwallis retreated to Georgia.

DIRECTIONS: Multiple Choice Indicate the answer choice that best completes the statement or answers the question.

_____ 6. Who led the Patriots' victory at Vincennes, which strengthened the American position in the West?

    A. Joseph Brant   **C.** Henry Hamilton

    B. George Rogers Clark   **D.** George Washington

_____ 7. Supplies and reinforcements could not reach American harbors because of

    A. a blockade.   **C.** lack of money.

    B. British spies.   **D.** Native Americans.

_____ 8. In March 1781, Nathanael Greene's forces met Charles Cornwallis's army at

    A. Charles Town.   **C.** Kings Mountain.

    B. Guilford Courthouse.   **D.** Savannah.

_____ 9. A merchant ship that is privately owned and armed with weapons is called a

    A. coastal warship.   **C.** merchant warship.

    B. garrison.   **D.** privateer.

_____ 10. The "Swamp Fox," known for his imaginative war tactics, was

    A. Benedict Arnold.   **C.** Francis Marion.

    B. George Rogers Clark.   **D.** George Washington.

Lesson Quiz 6-4

networks

The American Revolution

DIRECTIONS: Matching Match each item with the correct statement below.

_____ **1.** French commander

_____ **2.** British commander at Yorktown

_____ **3.** to approve officially

_____ **4.** September 3, 1783

_____ **5.** a surprise attack

A. Treaty of Paris

B. Comte de Rochambeau

C. Charles Cornwallis

D. ambush

E. ratify

DIRECTIONS: Multiple Choice Indicate the answer choice that best completes the statement or answers the question.

_____ **6.** Due to George Washington's strategy, Charles Cornwallis was defeated at the

    A. Battle of Boston.

    B. Battle of Chesapeake.

    C. Battle of New York.

    D. Battle of Yorktown.

_____ **7.** Although the last significant battle took place in 1781, the treaty ending the war was signed in

    A. 1781.

    B. 1783.

    C. 1787.

    D. 1800.

_____ **8.** The British recognized the United States as an independent nation in the

    A. Treaty of America.

    B. Treaty of Great Britain.

    C. Treaty of Paris.

    D. Treaty of the United States.

_____ **9.** Which foreign troops helped defeat British forces at Yorktown?

    A. African

    B. French

    C. German

    D. Spanish

_____ **10.** When Congress refused to pay soldiers who had won the American Revolution, conflict between the soldiers and Congress was resolved by

    A. John Adams.

    B. Benjamin Franklin.

    C. John Jay.

    D. George Washington.

Chapter 6 Test, Traditional

netw⊙rks

The American Revolution

DIRECTIONS: True/False Indicate whether the statement is true or false.

_____ **1.** The American colonies declared independence from Great Britain in July 1775.

_____ **2.** British advantages during the war included a stronger military, greater wealth, and a larger population.

_____ **3.** At least one-half of all American colonists were Tories.

_____ **4.** Most of the soldiers in the Continental Army signed up for the duration of the war.

_____ **5.** Nathan Hale was a Patriot soldier who became a traitor and spied for the British.

DIRECTIONS: Matching Match each term with the correct statement below.

_____ **6.** Patriot forces

_____ **7.** African American Patriot

_____ **8.** drilled Patriots at Valley Forge

_____ **9.** merchant warships

_____ **10.** hit-and-run war technique

A. Continental Army

B. Friedrich von Steuben

C. guerilla warfare

D. Lemuel Hayes

E. privateers

DIRECTIONS: Multiple Choice Indicate the answer choice that best completes the statement or answers the question.

_____ **11.** Where did the Patriot forces endure a winter of terrible suffering?
- **A.** Philadelphia
- **B.** Saratoga
- **C.** Valley Forge
- **D.** Yorktown

_____ **12.** Americans who remained loyal to Great Britain were called Loyalists or
- **A.** Colonists.
- **B.** Patriots.
- **C.** Separatists.
- **D.** Tories.

_____ **13.** By the end of the war, African Americans were enlisted in every state except

   A. Georgia.

   B. Maryland.

   C. North Carolina.

   D. South Carolina.

_____ **14.** Loyalist strength was strongest in

   A. New England.

   B. New York.

   C. the Carolinas and Georgia.

   D. the Ohio River Valley.

_____ **15.** The volunteer from France who became Washington's trusted aide was

   A. Benjamin Franklin.

   B. Francis Marion.

   C. Marquis de Lafayette.

   D. Thomas Paine.

_____ **16.** After the war, George Washington

   A. became a senator.

   B. moved to New York.

   C. ran for political office.

   D. returned to Mount Vernon.

"One saw men lying nearly everywhere who were mortally wounded and whose heads, arms, and legs had been shot off. . . . Likewise on watch and on post in the lines, on trench and work details, they were wounded by the fearfully heavy fire."

—Account by a Hessian soldier

_____ **17.** This excerpt describes the terrible effects of the battle at which Cornwallis surrendered. Which battle was it?

   A. Battle of Brandywine

   B. Battle of Camden

   C. Battle of Saratoga

   D. Battle of Yorktown

Chapter 6 Test, Traditional *cont.*

netw⚹rks

The American Revolution

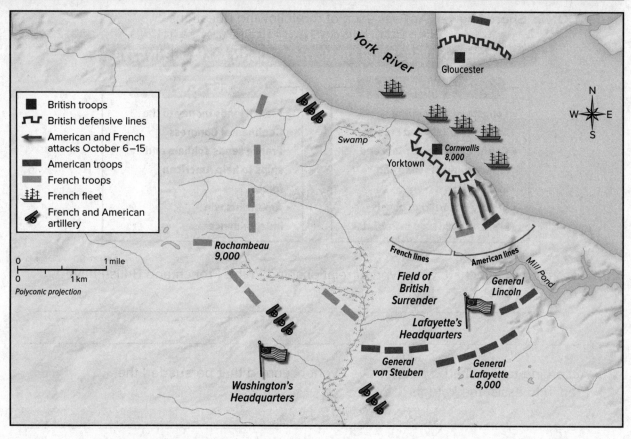

York River

Gloucester

British troops
British defensive lines
American and French attacks October 6–15
American troops
French troops
French fleet
French and American artillery

Swamp

Cornwallis 8,000

Yorktown

N
W⚹E
S

0   1 mile
0   1 km
Polyconic projection

Rochambeau 9,000

French lines

American lines

Mill Pond

Field of British Surrender

General Lincoln

Lafayette's Headquarters

General von Steuben

General Lafayette 8,000

Washington's Headquarters

_____ **18.** What is an appropriate title for this map?

    A. Battle at the Cape

    B. Battle of Yorktown

    C. Chesapeake Bay War

    D. Cornwallis Retreat

_____ **19.** Based on the map, the navy of which country played a decisive role at Yorktown?

    A. England

    B. France

    C. Canada

    D. United States

Chapter 6 Test, Traditional *cont.*

The American Revolution

DIRECTIONS: Short Answer Answer each of the following questions.

CAUSES AND EFFECTS OF FRENCH-AMERICAN ALLIANCE IN 1778

CAUSES	EFFECTS
• Longstanding hostility between Britain and France • Conflict between Britain and France during French and Indian War • Victory at Saratoga boosts French confidence in Patriots	• France lends money to the Continental Congress • France sends soldiers and ships to help American forces • Americans win independence

20. According to the chart, what type of relationship did the French and British have?

_____

_____

21. According to the chart, what positive event occurred that persuaded the French to assist the Patriots?

_____

_____

22. What is the name given to Americans who supported independence?

_____

23. What happened after Congress and the states printed hundreds of millions of dollars' worth of paper money to pay for the war?

_____

_____

DIRECTIONS: Essay Answer the following question on a separate piece of paper.

24. What were the Patriots' advantages in the war? The Patriots' disadvantages?

Discovering Our Past: A History of the United States

Chapter 6 Test, Document-Based Questions

The American Revolution

DIRECTIONS: Short Answer Answer each of the following questions.

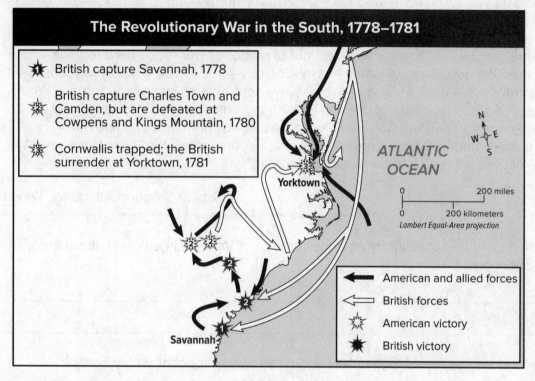

The Revolutionary War in the South, 1778–1781

1 British capture Savannah, 1778

2 British capture Charles Town and Camden, but are defeated at Cowpens and Kings Mountain, 1780

3 Cornwallis trapped; the British surrender at Yorktown, 1781

ATLANTIC OCEAN

Yorktown

Savannah

0   200 miles
0   200 kilometers
Lambert Equal-Area projection

→ American and allied forces
⇨ British forces
✴ American victory
✶ British victory

1. What is the name of the British commander who surrendered his forces at Yorktown, Virginia, in 1781?

   _____

2. What is the earliest event shown on this map?

   _____

3. According to the map, which three cities were captured by the British?

   _____

4. What do the white arrows on the map represent?

   _____

5. What is the last battle shown on the map?

   _____

Chapter 6 Test, Document-Based Questions *cont.*

networks

The American Revolution

> *"Dec. 14th.— . . .* The Army who have been surprisingly healthy hitherto—now begin to grow sickly from the continued fatigues they have suffered this Campaign. Yet they still show spirit of Alacrity & Contentment not to be expected from so young Troops. I am Sick—discontented—and out of humour. Poor food—hard lodging—Cold Weather—fatigue—Nasty Cloaths—nasty Cookery— . . . smoak'd out of my senses—the Devil's in't—I can't Endure it—Why are we sent here to starve and freeze—What sweet Felicities have I left at home;—A charming Wife—pretty Children—Good Beds—good food—good Cookery—all agreeable—all harmonious. Here, all Confusion—smoke Cold—hunger & filthyness—A pox on my bad luck. Here comes a bowl of beef soup—full of burnt leaves and dirt."
>
> —Diary of Surgeon Albigence Waldo

6. What does this account by an army surgeon at Valley Forge reveal about the Continental Army?

_____

_____

7. How does the army surgeon feel about this winter spent at Valley Forge?

_____

_____

8. What are some of the hardships described by the surgeon at Valley Forge?

_____

DIRECTIONS: Essay Answer the following question on a separate piece of paper.

9. Contrast the makeup of the American and British armies. Why did this difference favor the Americans?

Discovering Our Past: A History of the United States

Lesson Quiz 7-1

networks

A More Perfect Union

DIRECTIONS: Modified True/False In the blank, indicate whether the statement is true (T) or false (F). If false edit the statement to make it a true statement.

_____ **1.** By the end of 1776, all states had written their constitutions.

_____

_____ **2.** Americans were ready to concentrate power in the hands of a single ruler.

_____

_____ **3.** Under the Articles of Confederation, central government could carry out foreign affairs.

_____

DIRECTIONS: Multiple Choice Indicate the answer choice that best completes the statement or answers the question.

_____ **4.** The states adopted constitutions that limited the power of the

    A. governor.   **C.** state representative.

    B. president.   **D.** state senator.

_____ **5.** The Americans formed a republic, a government in which citizens rule through

    A. appointed representatives.   **C.** kingships.

    B. elected representatives.   **D.** monarchies.

_____ **6.** One of the Confederation's accomplishments was an arrangement for

    A. currency to be created.   **C.** new states in the West.

    B. foreign troops.   **D.** the military.

_____ **7.** What was the single territory that was created out of the lands north of the Ohio River and east of the Mississippi River?

    A. Mississippi Territory   **C.** Ohio Territory

    B. Northwest Territory   **D.** Western Territory

_____ **8.** One major weakness of the Confederation was that it could not deal with

    A. drawing maps.   **C.** new states.

    B. Native Americans.   **D.** the nation's finances.

Lesson Quiz 7-2

networks

A More Perfect Union

DIRECTIONS: Completion Enter the appropriate word(s) to complete the statement.

1. The United States went through an economic _____ after the American Revolution.

2. After hearing about _____, George Washington was willing to revise the Articles of Confederation.

3. Many white Southerners feared economic difficulties if _____ no longer existed.

4. The presence of George Washington and Benjamin Franklin guaranteed public trust in the _____.

5. In order to keep the Southern states part of the nation, Northern states agreed to prevent Congress from interfering with the slave trade until _____.

DIRECTIONS: Multiple Choice Indicate the answer choice that best completes the statement or answers the question.

_____ 6. Shays's Rebellion forced courts to close so judges could not take away

    A. criminals' homes.   **C.** stolen goods.

    B. farmers' land.   **D.** money from taxes.

_____ 7. The American Revolution brought into focus the contradiction between the American battle for liberty and

    A. the need for getting money.   **C.** women's right to vote.

    B. the practice of slavery.   **D.** the right of rebellion.

_____ 8. Constitutional Convention delegates voted to work toward a new national government based on the

    A. New Jersey Plan.   **C.** Northwest Territory Plan.

    B. New York Plan.   **D.** Virginia Plan.

_____ 9. Convention delegates broke the deadlock between large and small states when they approved

    A. the Great Compromise.

    B. the Three-Fifths Compromise.

    C. the Two-Thirds Compromise.

    D. the Washington Compromise.

Lesson Quiz 7-3

A More Perfect Union

networks

DIRECTIONS: Matching Match each item with the correct statement below.

_____ 1. Federalist

_____ 2. Anti-Federalist

_____ 3. checks and balances

_____ 4. Electoral College

_____ 5. Framers

A. favored local government controlled more closely by the people

B. the men who shaped the Constitution

C. supporter of the Constitution

D. system that keeps any one branch of government from gaining too much power

E. indirectly elects the president

DIRECTIONS: Multiple Choice Indicate the answer choice that best completes the statement or answers the question.

_____ 6. Those who opposed the Constitution feared the national government would

    A. limit the number of new states.

    B. limit trade.

    C. require religion to be practiced.

    D. take rights away from people.

_____ 7. The belief that all people have a right to life, liberty, and property was promoted by philosopher

    A. Baron de Montesquieu.   **C.** John Adams.

    B. Benjamin Franklin.   **D.** John Locke.

_____ 8. Which state was the last to ratify the Constitution?

    A. Maryland   **C.** North Carolina

    B. New York   **D.** Rhode Island

_____ 9. The branch of the government that is headed by the president is called the

    A. constitutional branch.   **C.** judicial branch.

    B. executive branch.   **D.** legislative branch.

_____ 10. The branch of government that deals with the court system is called the

    A. constitutional branch.   **C.** judicial branch.

    B. executive branch.   **D.** legislative branch.

Chapter 7 Test, Traditional

network

A More Perfect Union

DIRECTIONS: True/False Indicate whether the statement is true or false.

_____ **1.** After the American Revolution, most states allowed only white men who were at least 21 years old to vote.

_____ **2.** Slavery was a major source of labor in the North.

_____ **3.** The delegates at the Constitutional Convention included Native Americans, African Americans, and women.

_____ **4.** The first three articles of the Constitution describe the structure of the federal government.

_____ **5.** Anti-Federalists supported the Constitution.

DIRECTIONS: Matching Match each term with the correct statement below.

_____ **6.** manumission

_____ **7.** bicameral

_____ **8.** John Locke

_____ **9.** depreciate

_____ **10.** Roger Sherman

A. having two separate lawmaking chambers

B. to fall in value

C. the freeing of individual enslaved persons

D. proposed the Great Compromise

E. wrote that government is based on a contract between people and the ruler

DIRECTIONS: Multiple Choice Indicate the answer choice that best completes the statement or answers the question.

_____ **11.** Which law helped stop the spread of slavery to the West?

    A. Confederation Law

    B. Morris Ordinance

    C. Northwest Ordinance

    D. Ordinance of 1785

_____ **12.** The Articles of Confederation had to be approved by how many states?

    A. 7   **C.** 11

    B. 9   **D.** 13

_____ **13.** Who was the presiding officer at the Constitutional Convention?

    A. Benjamin Franklin   **C.** John Adams

    B. George Washington   **D.** Thomas Jefferson

Chapter 7 Test, Traditional *cont.*

A More Perfect Union

_____ **14.** Under the federal system of government, what or who is the final authority?

A. Constitution

C. president

B. court system

D. states

_____ **15.** The movement that influenced the Constitution's architects was the

A. Age of Science.

C. Ideas Period.

B. Enlightenment.

D. Reason Era.

Article II

"Each state retains its sovereignty, freedom, and independence, and every power, jurisdiction, and right, which is not . . . expressly delegated to the United States, in Congress assembled."

Article III

"The said States hereby severally enter into a firm league of friendship with each other, for their common defence, the security of their liberties, and their mutual and general welfare, binding themselves to assist each other against all force offered to, or attacks made upon them, or any of them, on account of religion, sovereignty, trade, or any other pretence whatever."

_____ **16.** This description of the "firm league of friendship" of states is a quotation from the

A. Articles of Association.

B. Articles of Confederation.

C. Constitution of the Republic.

D. Declaration of Federation.

_____ **17.** What does a "firm league of friendship" imply for the relationship of the states?

A. States can help one another only in desperate situations.

B. States can pick which states they want to help.

C. States can rely on another state only when it is beneficial for the states involved.

D. States must unite together to protect each other for their mutual well-being.

Discovering Our Past: A History of the United States

Chapter 7 Test, Traditional *cont.*

A More Perfect Union

> "[S]uerly your Honours are not Strangers to the Distresses of the people but . . . know That maney of our good Inhabitents are now Confined in gole [jail] for Debt and for taxes."
>
> —Petition from the town of Greenwich, Massachusetts

_____ **18.** Which uprising occurred when the petitions of the Massachusetts farmers, as stated in the quote, went unanswered?

    A. Boston Massacre

    B. Greenwich Revolt

    C. Shays's Rebellion

    D. Springfield's Uprising

> "[E]very Man has a *Property* in his own *Person*. This no Body has any Right to but himself."
>
> —*The Second Treatise of Government,* 1690

_____ **19.** The English philosopher John Locke is stating in this excerpt his belief in

    A. the right to vote.

    B. freedom of choice.

    C. the natural rights of people.

    D. the right to trade enslaved people.

> "The executive Power shall be vested in a President of the United States of America. He shall hold his Office during the Term of four Years, and, together with the Vice President, chosen for the same Term, be elected, as follows."
>
> — United States Constitution, Article II, Section 1 (ratified 1790)

_____ **20.** According to this excerpt, for how long does the vice president hold office?

    A. for life

    B. four years

    C. six years

    D. two terms

Chapter 7 Test, Traditional *cont.*

netw⊙rks

A More Perfect Union

DIRECTIONS: Short Answer Answer each of the following questions on a separate piece of paper.

21. What is the role of the executive branch?

FEDERAL AND STATE POWERS		
National Government	**National and State Governments**	**State Governments**
Coin money	Establish courts	Regulate trade within a state
Maintain army and navy	Enforce laws	Protect public welfare and safety
Declare war	Collect taxes	Conduct elections
Regulate trade between states and with foreign nations	Borrow money	Establish local governments
Carry out all expressed powers	Provide for general welfare	

22. According to the chart, who held the power to create money?

> "There is no declaration of rights; and, the laws of the general government being paramount to the laws and constitutions of the several states, the declarations of rights in the separate states are no security."
>
> —George Mason, 1787

23. Based on the excerpt, what was George Mason's view of individual states' bills of rights?

24. How was the Constitutional Convention organized?

25. What were the differences between the North and the South over slavery?

Chapter 7 Test, Document-Based Questions

networks

A More Perfect Union

DIRECTIONS: Short Answer Answer each of the following questions.

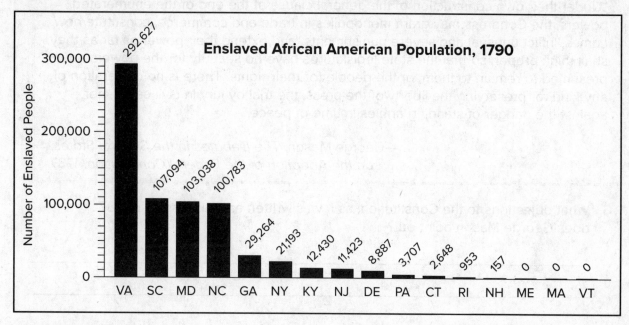

Enslaved African American Population, 1790

Number of Enslaved People

300,000 — 292,627

200,000

100,000 — 107,094 103,038 100,783

0 — 29,264 21,193 12,430 11,423 8,887 3,707 2,648 953 157 0 0 0

VA SC MD NC GA NY KY NJ DE PA CT RI NH ME MA VT

1. As shown in the graph, which state had the most enslaved African Americans? How many?

_____

2. Other than those states with zero enslaved African Americans, how many enslaved African Americans lived in the two states with the fewest enslaved people?

_____

3. Other than those states with zero enslaved African Americans, which two states had the biggest difference in the number of enslaved people living within their borders?

_____

4. According to the graph, how many enslaved African Americans lived in the two states with the most enslaved people?

_____

5. Which two states had the most similar numbers of enslaved people, as shown in the graph?

_____

"Under their own construction of the general clause at the end of the enumerated powers, the Congress may grant monopolies in trade and commerce, constitute new crimes, inflict unusual and severe punishments, and extend their power as far as they shall think proper; so that the state legislatures have no security for the powers now presumed to remain to them, or the people for their rights. There is no declaration of any kind for preserving the liberty of the press, the trial by jury in civil cases, nor against the danger of standing armies in time of peace."

—George Mason, *The Debates in the Several States,*
on the Adoption of the Federal Constitution, 1787

6. What objections to the Constitution, as it was written and discussed in 1787, does George Mason point out?

_____

_____

_____

_____

7. According to the excerpt, what are some actions that Congress was given the power to take?

_____

_____

_____

_____

DIRECTIONS: Essay Answer the following question on a separate piece of paper.

8. The graph and excerpt previously shown suggest that important changes were taking place in the United States during the late 1770s and 1780s. How did ideas about government and individual rights change during this period?

Lesson Quiz 8-1

networks

The Constitution

DIRECTIONS: Completion Enter the appropriate word(s) to complete the statement.

1. The first ten amendments added to the Constitution are known as the _____.

2. The words "We the People" are the first words of the _____.

3. If a state law _____ the Constitution or federal law, the Constitution or federal law prevails.

4. Ratified by the states in 1868, the Fourteenth Amendment granted full citizenship rights to _____.

5. The U.S. Congress claims _____, which are powers that are suggested but not directly stated in the Constitution.

DIRECTIONS: Multiple Choice Indicate the answer choice that best completes the statement or answers the question.

_____ 6. The Constitution, written in Philadelphia in 1787, included which of the following?

    A. Electoral College

    B. enumerated powers

    C. number of congressional districts

    D. number of Supreme Court justices

_____ 7. The Americans formed a republic, a government in which people rule through

    A. appointed representatives.   **C.** elected representatives.

    B. council of representatives.   **D.** popular vote.

_____ 8. The system established to maintain a balance of power between the three branches of government is called

    A. checks and balances.   **C.** separation of powers.

    B. equilibrium.   **D.** veto and override system.

_____ 9. For an amendment to be ratified, it must be approved by what fraction of the states?

    A. one-half   **C.** three-fourths

    B. one-third   **D.** nine-tenths

Discovering Our Past: A History of the United States

71

Lesson Quiz 8-2

networks

The Constitution

DIRECTIONS: True/False Indicate whether the statement is true or false.

_____ **1.** The president is head of the executive branch of the federal government.

_____ **2.** States with larger populations have more representatives in Congress.

_____ **3.** If at least one house of Congress agrees on a bill, the bill can be sent to the president.

_____ **4.** The term "U.S. soil" refers not only to the land of the United States but also to American territories and military bases around the world.

_____ **5.** The Fifth Amendment says no one shall "be deprived of life, liberty, or property, without due process of law."

DIRECTIONS: Multiple Choice Indicate the answer choice that best completes the statement or answers the question.

_____ **6.** A state's number of representatives may increase or decrease depending on changes to the

    A. economy.   **C.** population.

    B. Electoral College.   **D.** number of senators.

_____ **7.** Which of the following delegates to the House of Representatives is a voting member?

    A. District of Columbia   **C.** New Mexico

    B. Guam   **D.** Puerto Rico

_____ **8.** The Supreme Court has the power of

    A. filibuster.   **C.** judicial review.

    B. independent approval.   **D.** veto.

_____ **9.** A person who was born in another country can become a U.S. citizen through

    A. emigration.   **C.** naturalization.

    B. House approval.   **D.** Senate approval.

_____ **10.** How many justices make up the Supreme Court?

    A. eight   **C.** ten

    B. nine   **D.** twelve

Chapter 8 Test, Traditional

netw⊙rks

The Constitution

DIRECTIONS: True/False Indicate whether the statement is true or false.

_____ **1.** The Bill of Rights limits the power of government and protects the rights of individuals.

_____ **2.** The federal government reassigns each state's share of seats in the House of Representatives every two years.

_____ **3.** The main job of the executive branch of government is to administrate the laws passed by Congress.

_____ **4.** If a state law contradicts a federal law, the federal law prevails.

_____ **5.** The United States government cannot limit citizens' right to hold protests, even if public health or safety is at risk.

DIRECTIONS: Matching Match each item with the correct statement below.

_____ **6.** powers given specifically to Congress

_____ **7.** checks the power of Congress

_____ **8.** powers shared by the federal and state governments

_____ **9.** powers claimed by Congress but not directly stated in the Constitution

_____ **10.** powers that belong to the states alone

A. concurrent powers

B. enumerated powers

C. implied powers

D. reserved powers

E. veto power

DIRECTIONS: Multiple Choice Indicate the answer choice that best completes the statement or answers the question.

_____ **11.** For an amendment to be ratified, it must be approved by what fraction of the states?

    A. one-half

    B. three-fourths

    C. one-third

    D. nine-tenths

_____ **12.** The system set up to maintain a balance of power among the three branches of government is called

    A. checks and balances.

    B. equilibrium.

    C. separation of powers.

    D. veto and override system.

_____ **13.** The Constitution is based on how many key principles?

    A. three

    B. five

    C. seven

    D. nine

_____ **14.** Justices of the Supreme Court listen to legal arguments about a case and then present and explain a decision called

    A. the Court's opinion.

    B. the Final Rule.

    C. the Last Decree.

    D. the Supreme ruling.

_____ **15.** The process of changing the Constitution is started by

    A. a popular vote.

    B. the Congress.

    C. the president.

    D. the Supreme Court.

_____ **16.** There are no term limits for

    A. senators only.

    B. state representatives only.

    C. the president.

    D. both senators and state representatives.

Chapter 8 Test, Traditional *cont.*

netw🌐rks

The Constitution

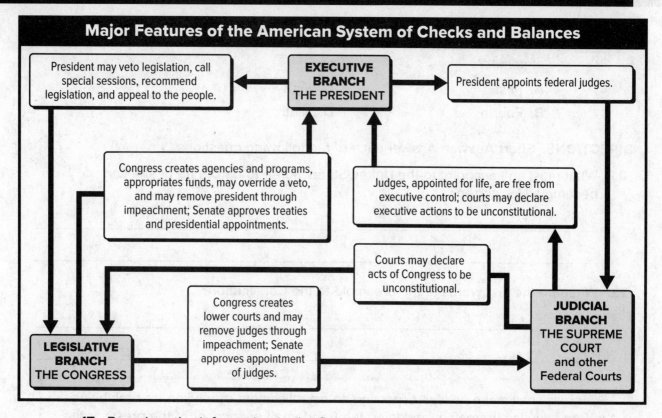

Major Features of the American System of Checks and Balances

President may veto legislation, call special sessions, recommend legislation, and appeal to the people.

EXECUTIVE BRANCH
THE PRESIDENT

President appoints federal judges.

Congress creates agencies and programs, appropriates funds, may override a veto, and may remove president through impeachment; Senate approves treaties and presidential appointments.

Judges, appointed for life, are free from executive control; courts may declare executive actions to be unconstitutional.

Courts may declare acts of Congress to be unconstitutional.

Congress creates lower courts and may remove judges through impeachment; Senate approves appointment of judges.

LEGISLATIVE BRANCH
THE CONGRESS

JUDICIAL BRANCH
THE SUPREME COURT
and other Federal Courts

_____ 17. Based on the information in the flowchart, which power does the executive branch have in legislation?

    A. power to declare unconstitutional

    B. power to impeach

    C. power to suspend

    D. power to veto

_____ 18. According to the flowchart, which entity can declare acts of Congress to be unconstitutional?

    A. executive

    B. judicial

    C. legislative

    D. president

_____ 19. Based on the information in the flowchart, which government officials are free from executive control?

    A. federal judges

    B. members of Congress

    C. senators

    D. state representatives

_____ **20.** Which amendment to the Constitution provides protections for people accused of crimes?

    A. First   **C.** Fifth

    B. Fourth   **D.** Ninth

DIRECTIONS: Short Answer Answer each of the following questions.

21. What must an immigrant to the United States agree to before he or she can become a U.S. citizen?

_____

_____

22. What are the first words of the preamble to the Constitution?

_____

_____

> "Congress shall make no law respecting an establishment of religion, or prohibiting the free exercise thereof; or abridging the freedom of speech, or of the press; or the right of the people peaceably to assemble, and to petition the Government for a redress of grievances."
>
> —United States Constitution, Amendment I

23. Rewrite this passage from the First Amendment in your own words.

_____

_____

24. From which part of the Constitution was this passage taken?

_____

_____

25. Do you believe that one branch of the United States government is more important than the others? Why or why not?

_____

_____

Chapter 8 Test, Document-Based Questions

network

The Constitution

DIRECTIONS: Multiple Choice Indicate the answer choice that best completes the statement or answers the question.

> "You must first enable the government to control the governed; and in the next place oblige it to control itself."
>
> —James Madison

_____ **1.** James Madison introduced the Bill of Rights to protect

   A. national government.

   B. personal liberties.

   C. unlimited state power.

   D. the Constitution.

> "No person shall be held to answer for a capital, or otherwise infamous crime, unless on a presentment or indictment of a Grand Jury, except in cases arising in the land or naval forces, or in the Militia, when in actual service in time of War or public danger; nor shall any person be subject for the same offence to be twice put in jeopardy of life or limb; nor shall be compelled in any criminal case to be a witness against himself, nor be deprived of life, liberty, or property, without due process of law; nor shall private property be taken for public use, without just compensation."

_____ **2.** Which amendment of the Constitution provides protections for people accused of crimes?

   A. First Amendment

   B. Fourth Amendment

   C. Fifth Amendment

   D. Ninth Amendment

Chapter 8 Test, Document-Based Questions *cont.*

The Constitution

DIRECTIONS: Short Answer Answer each of the following questions on a separate piece of paper.

MAJOR PRINCIPLES OF THE CONSTITUTION	
Popular Sovereignty	People are the source of the government's power.
Republicanism	People elect their political representatives.
Limited Government	The Constitution limits the actions of government by specifically listing powers it does and does not have.
Federalism	In this government system, power is divided between national and state governments.
Separation of Powers	Each of the three branches of government has its own responsibilities.
Checks and Balances	Each branch of government holds some control over the other two branches.
Individual Rights	Basic liberties and rights of all citizens are guaranteed in the Bill of Rights.

3. Study the chart. Which major principle of the Constitution addresses the issue of government control over its three branches?

4. Study the chart. How does the Constitution limit government?

5. What is "popular sovereignty"?

6. Study the chart. Which major principle of the Constitution provides that there are two levels of government within the United States?

DIRECTIONS: Essay Answer the following question on a separate piece of paper.

7. Why was the government of the United States formed?

Lesson Quiz 9-1

The Federalist Era

DIRECTIONS: Multiple Choice Indicate the answer choice that best completes the statement or answers the question.

_____ 1. Who was the nation's first vice president?

    A. Benjamin Franklin   **C.** John Adams

    B. George Washington   **D.** Samuel Adams

_____ 2. What is one of the liberties guaranteed in the Bill of Rights?

    A. freedom of speech   **C.** right to own a home

    B. freedom to ban the press   **D.** right to refuse to pay taxes

_____ 3. Who was the first chief justice of the United States?

    A. Alexander Hamilton   **C.** John Adams

    B. George Washington   **D.** John Jay

_____ 4. The Judiciary Act of 1789 established which kind of legal system?

    A. congressional law system   **C.** international court system

    B. federal court system   **D.** stack court system

_____ 5. To help build a strong national economy, what did Hamilton ask Congress to create?

    A. a national bank   **C.** trade tariffs

    B. the stock market   **D.** Washington, D.C.

DIRECTIONS: Short Answer Answer each of the following questions.

6. What is a "precedent"?

_____

7. Within the executive branch, what did the three department heads and the attorney general come to be known as?

_____

8. Who was the first leader of the new Department of State?

_____

9. What act of Congress established a federal court system?

_____

10. What or who is a "speculator"?

_____

Discovering Our Past: A History of the United States

Lesson Quiz 9-2

networks

The Federalist Era

DIRECTIONS: Matching Match each item with the correct statement below.

_____ **1.** tax protest

_____ **2.** diplomat

_____ **3.** not taking sides

_____ **4.** forced into British navy

_____ **5.** agreement with Spain

A. neutrality

B. Whiskey Rebellion

C. Pinckney's Treaty

D. Edmond Genêt

E. impressment

DIRECTIONS: Multiple Choice Indicate the answer choice that best completes the statement or answers the question.

_____ **6.** In which region of the country did taxes on whiskey lead to a rebellion?

    A. Boston

    B. Oregon country

    C. Virginia

    D. western Pennsylvania

_____ **7.** Around 1794, where did the British begin building a new fort?

    A. Kentucky   **C.** Ohio

    B. New York   **D.** Virginia

_____ **8.** Which treaty opened most of Ohio to white settlers?

    A. Jay's Treaty   **C.** Treaty of Greenville

    B. Pinckney's Treaty   **D.** Treaty of Ohio

_____ **9.** What barred French and British warships from American ports?

    A. Declaration of War

    B. Proclamation of Neutrality

    C. Treaty of Britain

    D. Treaty of Paris

_____ **10.** What did George Washington consider a grave danger to the new nation?

    A. France's influence

    B. growth of political parties

    C. national taxes

    D. settlers moving west

Discovering Our Past: A History of the United States

Lesson Quiz 9-3

networks

The Federalist Era

DIRECTIONS: Completion Enter the appropriate word(s) to complete the statement.

1. Many Americans agreed with George Washington's belief that _____ were harmful to good government.

2. The _____ party admired Britain's stability.

3. To favor one side of an issue is to be _____.

4. President Adams referred to the three French agents who demanded a bribe and a loan from the Americans as _____.

5. According to Federalist Party leaders, the _____ Acts, passed in 1798, would protect the nation's security.

DIRECTIONS: Multiple Choice Indicate the answer choice that best completes the statement or answers the question.

_____ 6. Which political party stood for a strong federal government?

   A. Anti-Federalist   **C.** Democratic-Republican

   B. Democratic   **D.** Federalist

_____ 7. Which party feared that a strong central government would endanger people's liberties?

   A. Anti-Federalist   **C.** Federalist

   B. Democratic   **D.** Republican

_____ 8. Who was the second president of the United States?

   A. Aaron Burr   **C.** John Adams

   B. Charles Pinckney   **D.** Thomas Jefferson

_____ 9. Which of the following proposed a challenge to the constitutional authority of the national government?

   A. peace with France

   B. political parties

   C. Sedition Act

   D. Virginia and Kentucky Resolutions

_____ 10. What divided the Federalists and hurt John Adams's chance for reelection?

   A. Neutrality Act   **C.** treaty with France

   B. states' rights   **D.** war with France

Discovering Our Past: A History of the United States

Chapter 9 Test, Traditional

networks

The Federalist Era

DIRECTIONS: True/False Indicate whether the statement is true or false.

_____ **1.** During the Whiskey Rebellion, farmers peacefully protested a special tax.

_____ **2.** Native Americans often turned to Britain and Spain for help in preventing Americans from settling in the West.

DIRECTIONS: Multiple Choice Indicate the answer choice that best completes the statement or answers the question.

> ". . . [A]n assumption of the debts of the particular States by the Union, and a like provision for them as for those of the Union, will be a measure of sound policy and substantial justice.
>
> "It would, in the opinion of the Secretary, contribute, in an eminent degree, to an orderly, stable, and satisfactory arrangement of the national finances. . . . [N]o greater revenues will be required whether that provision be made wholly by the United States, or partly by them and partly by the States separately. . . .
>
> "If all the public creditors receive their dues from one source, distributed with an equal hand, their interest will be the same. And, having the same interests, they will unite in the support of the fiscal arrangements of the Government . . . These circumstances combined will insure to the revenue laws a more ready and more satisfactory execution. . . ."
>
> —Alexander Hamilton, "Report on the Public Credit," January 1790

_____ **3.** In this excerpt, what does Alexander Hamilton argue that the new United States government should do?

    A. pay off only Confederation government debts to foreign countries

    B. pay off only Confederation debts to individual citizens

    C. pay off the Confederation government's debts

    D. refuse to pay debts from the Revolutionary War

_____ **4.** What does Alexander Hamilton believe will happen if all public creditors are paid equally?

    A. They will reinvest their money in the government.

    B. They will support the government's management of national finances.

    C. They will support the Federalist Party

    D. They will support the Republican Party.

CONFLICT BETWEEN THE UNITED STATES AND FRANCE

French begin seizing American ships.

↓

President John Adams sends negotiators to France.

↓

French agents demand loan and bribe.

↓

United States strengthens military forces.

↓

United States and France engage in undeclared war.

_____ **5.** Why did President Adams send negotiators to France?

   A. French agents demanded a loan and a bribe.

   B. The French had begun capturing American ships.

   C. to say to the French that the United States was strengthening its army.

   D. United States and France were involved in an undeclared war.

_____ **6.** What was the United States reaction to the French agents' demand for a loan and a bribe?

   A. United States began capturing French ships.

   B. United States declared war on France.

   C. United States established new negotiations with France.

   D. United States strengthened its army.

_____ **7.** What was the name of the civil uprising against the taxing power of the federal government?

   A. Battle of Fallen Timbers

   B. Tea Party Rebellion

   C. XYZ affair

   D. Whiskey Rebellion

_____ **8.** The Alien and Sedition Acts were

    A. strongly supported by the Republican Party.

    B. passed to increase immigration.

    C. strongly supported by the Federalist Party.

    D. passed to strengthen the nation's military.

_____ **9.** The Proclamation of Neutrality barred which warships from American ports?

    A. French and English

    B. German and English

    C. Italian and Spanish

    D. Spanish and Portuguese

_____ **10.** Who expressed concern that political parties were a threat to the ability of people in government to work together?

    A. Alexander Hamilton   **C.** John Adams

    B. George Washington   **D.** Thomas Jefferson

_____ **11.** Whose forces were defeated by Little Turtle in 1791?

    A. Anthony Wayne

    B. General Arthur St. Clair

    C. General George Washington

    D. John Jay

_____ **12.** What did the Virginia and Kentucky Resolutions claim?

    A. The Alien and Sedition Acts violated the Constitution.

    B. Jay's Treaty violated the Constitution.

    C. Pinckney's Treaty was biased in favor of wealthy landowners.

    D. Settlers had the right to settle in the Northwest Territories.

DIRECTIONS: Short Answer Answer each of the following questions on a separate piece of paper.

13. Whose forces were defeated by Anthony Wayne in the Battle of Fallen Timbers?

14. Why was Jay's Treaty unpopular?

"The support of government—the support of troops for the common defense—the payment of the public debt, are the true *final causes* for raising money. The disposition and regulation of it, when raised, are the steps by which it is applied to the *ends* for which it was raised, . . . Hence, therefore, the money to be raised by taxes, as well as any other personal property, must be supposed to come within the meaning, as they certainly do within the letter, of authority to make all needful rules and regulations concerning the property of the United States. . . .

"... [A national] bank has a natural relation to the power of collecting taxes—to that of regulating trade—to that of providing for the common defense—and that, as the bill under consideration contemplates the government in the light of a joint proprietor of the stock of the bank it brings the case within the provision of the clause of the Constitution which immediately respects the property of the United States. . . ."

— Alexander Hamilton, "On the Constitutionality of
the Bank of the United States"

15. What is a reason given for the creation of the national bank?

"Congress shall make no law respecting an establishment of religion, or prohibiting the free exercise thereof; or abridging the freedom of speech, or of the press; or the right of the people peaceably to assemble, and to petition the Government for a redress of grievances."

—United States Constitution, Amendment I

16. What does the First Amendment say about freedom of speech?

17. How did the administration that took office in 1797 come to have a Federalist president and a Republican vice president?

Chapter 9 Test, Document-Based Questions

The Federalist Era

DIRECTIONS: Short Answer Answer each of the following questions on a separate piece of paper.

> ". . . To the efficacy and permanency of your union a government for the whole is indispensable. No alliances, however strict, between the parts can be an adequate substitute. They must inevitably experience the infractions and interruptions which all alliances in all times have experienced. Sensible of this momentous truth, you have improved upon your first essay [try] by the adoption of a Constitution of Government better calculated than your former for an intimate union and for the efficacious management of your common concerns. This Government, the offspring of our own choice, uninfluenced and unawed, adopted upon full investigation and mature deliberation, completely free in its principles, in the distribution of its powers, uniting security with energy, and containing within itself a provision for its own amendment, has a just claim to your confidence and your support. . . ."
>
> —George Washington, "Farewell Address," September 1796

1. To what does Washington refer when he says "you have improved upon your first essay" in this excerpt from his "Farewell Address"?

2. Which improvements does Washington note?

> "No person shall be held to answer for a capital, or otherwise infamous crime, unless on a presentment or indictment of a Grand Jury, except in cases arising in the land or naval forces, or in the Militia, when in actual service in time of War or public danger; nor shall any person be subject for the same offence to be twice put in jeopardy of life or limb; nor shall be compelled in any criminal case to be a witness against himself, nor be deprived of life, liberty, or property, without due process of law; nor shall private property be taken for public use without just compensation."
>
> —United States Constitution, Amendment V

3. According to this amendment, how many times can a person be tried for the same offense?

4. What are the exceptions to the law stated in this amendment?

Chapter 9 Test, Document-Based
Questions *cont.*

The Federalist Era

> "The enumeration in the Constitution, of certain rights, shall not be construed to deny or disparage others retained by the people."
>
> —United States Constitution, Amendment IX

5. What does the Ninth Amendment, quoted here, prevent from happening?

> " . . . Persuaded, as the Secretary is, that the proper funding of the present debt will render it a national blessing, yet he is so far from acceding to [agreeing with] the position, in the latitude in which it is sometimes laid down, that 'public debts are public benefits'—a position inviting to prodigality [extravagance] and liable to dangerous abuse—that he ardently wishes to see it incorporated as a fundamental maxim in the system of public credit of the United States, that the creation of debt should always be accompanied with the means of extinguishment."
>
> —Alexander Hamilton, Report as Secretary of the Treasury, 1790

6. In this excerpt from his report in 1790, Alexander Hamilton, the U.S. secretary of the treasury, felt strongly about what in terms of the national debt?

Discovering Our Past: A History of the United States

Lesson Quiz 10-1

networks

The Jefferson Era

DIRECTIONS: Completion Enter the appropriate word(s) to complete the statement.

1. In the election of 1800, Federalists supported _____ for a second term.

2. Congress passed the _____ to prevent another showdown between a presidential and a vice-presidential candidate.

3. Under Jefferson, all government funds would come from the sale of western lands and taxes on imported goods called _____.

4. Jefferson and Gallatin worked on reducing the _____.

5. The last-minute judicial appointments by Adams were called _____.

DIRECTIONS: Multiple Choice Indicate the answer choice that best completes the statement or answers the question.

_____ 6. The election of 1800 was decided by

    A. the Senate.   **C.** the Electoral College.

    B. the popular vote.   **D.** the House of Representatives.

_____ 7. Regional courts were set up for the United States with the

    A. Judiciary Act of 1801.   **C.** Marshall Supreme Court.

    B. *Marbury* v. *Madison* case.   **D.** midnight judges.

_____ 8. Which case represented the first time the Supreme Court reviewed and ruled on acts of the other branches of government?

    A. *Adams* v. *Jefferson*   **C.** *Marbury* v. *Madison*

    B. *Jefferson* v. *Madison*   **D.** *Marshall* v. *Madison*

_____ 9. Jefferson believed in reducing the power and size of government, or a philosophy called

    A. federalism.   **C.** *laissez-faire.*

    B. judicial review.   **D.** states' rights.

_____ 10. Who had John Adams named to serve as chief justice of the Supreme Court?

    A. Aaron Burr   **C.** John Marshall

    B. George Washington   **D.** Thomas Jefferson

Lesson Quiz 10-2

netw⊚rks

The Jefferson Era

DIRECTIONS: True/False Indicate whether the statement is true or false.

_____ 1. Jefferson believed that French control of the Louisiana Territory would improve American trade on the Mississippi River.

_____ 2. The revolt in Saint Domingue had an effect on France's plans in the United States.

_____ 3. After 18 months, the Lewis and Clark expedition reached the Pacific Ocean.

_____ 4. Lewis and Clark's expedition collected valuable information on people, plants, and animals.

_____ 5. A group of Republicans plotted to secede from the Union.

DIRECTIONS: Multiple Choice Indicate the answer choice that best completes the statement or answers the question.

_____ 6. Before it was transferred in 1802, the Louisiana Territory belonged to

    A. England.   **C.** Louisiana.

    B. France.   **D.** Spain.

_____ 7. After it was secretly transferred in 1802, the Louisiana Territory belonged to

    A. England.   **C.** Spain.

    B. France.   **D.** the United States.

_____ 8. The size of the United States was doubled with

    A. the adoption of New Orleans.

    B. the expedition of Lewis and Clark.

    C. the Louisiana Purchase.

    D. Zebulon Pike's expedition.

_____ 9. The Grand Peak was named by the explorer

    A. Meriwether Lewis.   **C.** William Clark.

    B. Sacagawea.   **D.** Zebulon Pike.

_____ 10. Which politician died as a result of a duel?

    A. Aaron Burr   **C.** John Adams

    B. Alexander Hamilton   **D.** Thomas Jefferson

Lesson Quiz 10-3

networks

The Jefferson Era

DIRECTIONS: True/False Indicate whether the statement is true or false.

_____ **1.** The Barbary Coast states of North Africa included Morocco and Tripoli.

_____ **2.** Neutrality is the ability to choose sides during a war.

_____ **3.** The 1807 Embargo Act prohibited trade with other countries.

_____ **4.** The capital of the confederation of Native American nations was Prophetstown.

_____ **5.** The War Hawks wanted war for more than one reason.

DIRECTIONS: Short Answer Answer each of the following questions.

6. How did the war between France and Britain in the mid-1790s affect American business?

_____

_____

_____

7. Which Barbary Coast state declared war on the United States in 1801?

_____

8. Which event enraged Americans in 1807?

_____

_____

9. Who was the Shawnee chief who built a confederacy among Native American nations?

_____

10. Who were the two War Hawks who led the push for war with Britain?

_____

Lesson Quiz 10-4

networks

The Jefferson Era

DIRECTIONS: Matching Match each item with the correct statement below.

_____ **1.** commander of Lake Erie naval forces

A. Francis Scott Key

_____ **2.** frigates

B. Andrew Jackson

_____ **3.** wrote the national anthem

C. privateers

_____ **4.** armed private ships

D. warships

_____ **5.** attacked the Creeks

E. Oliver Hazard Perry

DIRECTIONS: Multiple Choice Indicate the answer choice that best completes the statement or answers the question.

_____ **6.** The great leader Tecumseh was killed in the

    A. Battle of Lake Erie.

    B. Battle of the Thames.

    C. Battle of Tippecanoe.

    D. Battle of Toronto.

_____ **7.** With the death of Tecumseh, hopes died for

    A. a Native American victory.

    B. a Native American confederation.

    C. the movement of white settlers.

    D. the Native American revolt.

_____ **8.** One of the buildings burned by the British was

    A. the Capitol.   **C.** the Patent Office.

    B. Mount Vernon.   **D.** Washington Manor.

_____ **9.** "The Star-Spangled Banner" was written by

    A. Andrew Jackson.   **C.** George Washington.

    B. Francis Scott Key.   **D.** Thomas Jefferson.

_____ **10.** Which battle made Andrew Jackson a national hero and eventually helped him win the presidency?

    A. Battle of Lake Erie

    B. Battle of the Bulge

    C. Battle of New Orleans

    D. Battle of the Thames

Chapter 10 Test, Traditional

networks

The Jefferson Era

DIRECTIONS: True/False Indicate whether the statement is true or false.

_____ **1.** The Native Americans were allies of the British in the War of 1812.

_____ **2.** The War of 1812 ended with the Treaty of Tecumseh.

_____ **3.** In 1800 the United States claimed the area west of the Mississippi River.

_____ **4.** The revolution in Santo Domingo led to Napoleon selling the Louisiana Territory.

_____ **5.** The Louisiana Territory was purchased under the presidential administration of Thomas Jefferson.

DIRECTIONS: Matching Match each item with the correct statement below.

_____ **6.** tribute   **A.** the Prophet

_____ **7.** United States Navy captain   **B.** protection money

_____ **8.** powerful Shawnee leader   **C.** William Henry Harrison

_____ **9.** Tecumseh's brother and ally   **D.** Stephen Decatur

_____ **10.** attacked Prophetstown   **E.** Tecumseh

DIRECTIONS: Multiple Choice Indicate the answer choice that best completes the statement or answers the question.

_____ **11.** The leading War Hawks were

    A. Calhoun and Harrison.

    B. Clay and Calhoun.

    C. Clay and Tecumseh.

    D. Decatur and Pinckney.

_____ **12.** Which British practice was a violation of neutral rights?

    A. embargoes

    B. impressment

    C. smuggling

    D. U.S. trading

_____ **13.** Tecumseh joined forces with Great Britain after the

    A. Battle of Tippecanoe.

    B. Confederacy of Ohio.

    C. Treaty of Prophetstown.

    D. War of Tripoli.

_____ **14.** The Supreme Court reviewing and ruling on acts of other branches of the government is called

    A. judicial review.

    B. law review.

    C. supremacy.

    D. Supreme ruling.

_____ **15.** Which commander destroyed the British naval forces on Lake Erie?

    A. Andrew Jackson

    B. Oliver Hazard Perry

    C. James Madison

    D. William Hull

> "The country is as yesterday beatifull in the extreme."
>
> —Meriwether Lewis, Journal Entry, May 5, 1805

_____ **16.** Which country is Lewis referring to in this excerpt from his journals?

    A. Canada

    B. Mexico

    C. the Louisiana Territory

    D. the Ohio Territory

> "O! say can you see by the dawn's early light,
>
> What so proudly we hailed at the twilight's last gleaming,
>
> Whose broad stripes and bright stars through the perilous fight,
>
> O'er the ramparts we watch'd, were so gallantly streaming?
>
> And the Rockets' red glare, the Bombs bursting in air,
>
> Gave proof through the night that our Flag was still there."
>
> —"The Star-Spangled Banner," 1812

_____ **17.** From which harbor did Francis Scott Key, the author of this song, watch anxiously through the night of September 13–14 the bombardment from Fort McHenry?

    A. Baltimore, Maryland

    B. Charleston, South Carolina

    C. Philadelphia, Pennsylvania

    D. Washington, D.C.

> "May the Lord bless King George, convert him, and take him to heaven, as we want no more of him."
>
> —Reverend John Gruber, to his Baltimore congregation, 1814

_____ **18.** The Reverend Gruber offered this blessing during which war?

    A. the American Revolution

    B. the French and Indian War

    C. the Spanish–American War

    D. the War of 1812

_____ **19.** What decided the election of 1800?

    A. the Electoral College

    B. the House of Representatives

    C. the popular vote

    D. the Senate

_____ **20.** What was one of the goals of Lewis and Clark's expedition?

    A. to build schools and hospitals

    B. to deliver documents to French officials

    C. to establish trade with Canada

    D. to find and map the Northwest Passage

DIRECTIONS: Short Answer Answer each of the following questions on a separate piece of paper.

> "The gentleman who was to give the word then explained to the parties the rules which were to govern them in firing. . . . He then asked if they were prepared; being answered in the affirmative, he gave the word *present*, as had been agreed on, and both parties presented and fired in succession. . . . The fire of Colonel Burr took effect, and General Hamilton almost instantly fell. Colonel Burr advanced towards General Hamilton with a manner and gesture that appeared to General Hamilton's friend to be expressive of regret."
>
> — Account by Matthew Davis of the Burr-Hamilton Duel, July 1804

21. What was the outcome of the duel?

"*Nov. 7, 1805.* A cloudy foggey morning. Some rain. We set out early, proceeded under the stard. [starboard] side under high ruged hills with steep assent, the shore boalt and rockey, the fog so thick we could not see across the river. Two canos of Indians met and returned with us to their village which is situated on the stard. side behind a cluster of marshey islands, on a narrow chanl. of the river through which we passed to the village of 4 houses. They gave us to eate some fish, and sold us fish, *wap pa to* roots, three dogs and 2 otter skins for which we gave fish hooks principally, of which they were verry fond. . . .

"After delaying at this village one hour and a half we set out piloted by an Indian dressed in a salors dress, to the main chanel of the river. The tide being in we should have found much dificuelty in passing into the main chanel from behind those islands, without a pilot."

—William Clark, journals of the Lewis and Clark Expedition, 1804–1806

22. In this excerpt, what is William Clark's view of the Native Americans he encounters?

23. What political unrest did the Louisiana Purchase cause?

24. Instead of traveling around the country to gain support as in today's elections, how did the candidates campaign for the election of 1800?

DIRECTIONS: Essay Answer the following question on a separate piece of paper.

25. Why did the Embargo Act of 1807 divide the American people?

Chapter 10 Test, Document-Based Questions   networks

The Jefferson Era

DIRECTIONS: Multiple Choice Indicate the answer choice that best answers the question.

The Louisiana Purchase		
State	**Area in Square Miles**	**Date of Statehood**
Arkansas	53,104	June 15, 1836
Colorado	104,247	August 1, 1876
Iowa	56,290	December 28, 1846
Kansas	82,264	January 29, 1861
Louisiana	48,523	April 30, 1812
Minnesota	84,068	May 11, 1858
Missouri	69,686	August 10, 1821
Montana	147,138	November 8, 1889
Nebraska	77,138	March 1, 1867
North Dakota	70,665	November 2, 1889
Oklahoma	69,919	November 16, 1907
South Dakota	77,047	November 2, 1889
Wyoming	97,914	July 10, 1890

_____ **1.** Based on the chart, which two states from the Louisiana Purchase are the largest in size?

    A. Colorado and Montana

    B. Colorado and Oklahoma

    C. Wyoming and Colorado

    D. Wyoming and Montana

Chapter 10 Test, Document-Based Questions *cont.*

The Jefferson Era

DIRECTIONS: Short Answer Answer each of the following questions.

> "[O]nce, nor until lately, there was no white man on this continent. That it then all belonged to red men, children of the same parents, placed on it by the Great Spirit that made them, to keep it, to traverse it, to enjoy its productions, and to fill it with the same race. Once a happy race. Since made miserable by the white people, who are never contented, but always encroaching. The way, and the only way to check and stop this evil, is, for all the red men to unite in claiming a common and equal right in the land, as it was at first, and should be yet; for it never was divided, but belongs to all, for the use of each. That no part has a right to sell, even to each other, much less to strangers, those who want all, and will not do with less. The white people have no right to take the land from the Indians, because they had it first; it is theirs. They may sell, but all must join. Any sale not made by all is not valid. The late sale is bad. It was made by a part only."
>
> —Tecumseh, Shawnee leader

2. According to the passage, how does Tecumseh view the sale of land?

_____

_____

3. What does Tecumseh mean by the phrase, "the white people, who are never contented, but always encroaching"?

_____

_____

4. Why does Tecumseh say the white man has no right to the land?

_____

_____

DIRECTIONS: Essay Answer the following question on a separate piece of paper.

5. Describe the role of Native Americans in the War of 1812.

Lesson Quiz 11-1

networks

Growth and Expansion

DIRECTIONS: True/False Indicate whether the statement is true or false.

_____ **1.** The period in history when many people left their homes and farms to work in mills was called the Industrial Revolution.

_____ **2.** New England offered ideal conditions for farming.

_____ **3.** A patent gives a person legal rights regarding an invention.

_____ **4.** Corporations developed rapidly in the 1830s when legal obstacles to their formation were removed.

_____ **5.** Libraries, museums, and a variety of shops were in plentiful supply in rural America in the 1800s.

DIRECTIONS: Multiple Choice Indicate the answer choice that best answers the question.

_____ **6.** What was at the heart of the Industrial Revolution?

    A. the cotton gin

    B. new machines and new technology

    C. farms, rivers, and streams

    D. the steam generator

_____ **7.** What was a significant development in the way goods were made?

    A. development of mills

    B. economic factors

    C. factory system

    D. wealthy merchant association

_____ **8.** What helped increase cotton production?

    A. cotton gin

    B. cotton mill

    C. factory system

    D. steam generator

_____ **9.** In what area did many new industrial towns develop?

    A. along mountain ranges

    B. near oceans and bays

    C. near other large towns

    D. along rivers and streams

Discovering Our Past: A History of the United States

Lesson Quiz 11-2

networks

Growth and Expansion

DIRECTIONS: Completion Enter the appropriate word(s) to complete the statement.

1. The first census of the United States was taken in the year _____.

2. The _____ extended from New York City to Buffalo and was 363 miles long.

3. Beginning in the 1780s, _____ engines were used to power boats.

4. A series of _____ along a canal work like an escalator to help raise and lower boats up and down hills.

5. Pioneer women in the West would get together for _____ parties.

DIRECTIONS: Multiple Choice Indicate the answer choice that best answers the question.

_____ 6. What were roads consisting of logs laid side by side called?

    A. corduroy roads

    B. cotton roads

    C. ridge roads

    D. silk roads

_____ 7. Which road connected Ohio with the East?

    A. East-West Road

    B. National Road

    C. Ohio Road

    D. Vandalia Road

_____ 8. Where did early pioneer families tend to settle in communities?

    A. along canals

    B. along great rivers

    C. along state borders

    D. along toll roads

_____ 9. Which of these means of transportation contributed to the growth of river cities such as Cincinnati?

    A. canals

    B. Conestoga wagons

    C. new roads

    D. steamboats

Discovering Our Past: A History of the United States

Lesson Quiz 11-3

netw⊙rks

Growth and Expansion

DIRECTIONS: Matching Match each item with the correct statement below.

_____ **1.** loyalty to a region

A. John Marshall

_____ **2.** building of roads, bridges, and canals

B. sectionalism

_____ **3.** chief justice of Supreme Court

C. Adams-Onís Treaty

_____ **4.** gave control of Florida to the United States

D. Henry Clay

_____ **5.** nicknamed "The Great Compromiser"

E. internal improvements

DIRECTIONS: Multiple Choice Indicate the answer choice that best answers the question.

_____ **6.** What happened as a result of the formation of the Second Bank of the United States?

   A. American businesses were able to grow.

   B. Many state banks acted unwisely.

   C. Republicans closed the bank.

   D. Too much money was in circulation.

_____ **7.** Why did the period of national harmony end?

   A. because of arguments over the flag

   B. because of arguments over war

   C. because of political parties

   D. because of regional differences

_____ **8.** How was the balance between the North and the South preserved in the Senate?

   A. by the Maine Compromise

   B. by the Missouri Compromise

   C. by the North-South Compromise

   D. by the Ohio Compromise

_____ **9.** Which of the following called for a stop to European colonization of the Americas?

   A. Adams-Onís Treaty

   B. Convention of 1818

   C. Monroe Doctrine

   D. Rush-Bagot Treaty

NAME_____ DATE _____ CLASS _____

Chapter 11 Test, Traditional   **networks**

Growth and Expansion

DIRECTIONS: True/False Indicate whether the statement is true or false.

_____ **1.** In a capitalist system, the government owns property and decides how to use it.

_____ **2.** Daniel Boone, an early western pioneer, explored a Native American trail through the Appalachian Mountains.

_____ **3.** The National Road helped connect the new state of Ohio with the South.

_____ **4.** James Monroe faced many Federalist candidates during the 1816 presidential election.

_____ **5.** Miguel Hidalgo led the movement for independence in Venezuela and Colombia.

DIRECTIONS: Matching Match each item with the correct statement below.

_____ **6.** official count of the population   **A.** Lowell girls

_____ **7.** factory workers   **B.** Eli Whitney

_____ **8.** kept an even balance of power in the Senate   **C.** census

_____ **9.** invented cotton gin   **D.** Robert Fulton

_____ **10.** designed the *Clermont*   **E.** Missouri Compromise

DIRECTIONS: Multiple Choice Indicate the answer choice that best completes the statement or answers the question.

> "If thou canst do this thing, I invite thee to come to Rhode Island, and have the credit of introducing cotton manufacture into America."
>
> —letter from Moses Brown, 1789

_____ **11.** Who is the recipient of this letter who memorized the design of British machines and duplicated them in Rhode Island?

    A. Eli Whitney   **C.** Lucy Larcom

    B. Francis Cabot Lowell   **D.** Samuel Slater

_____ **12.** According to the quote, what benefit would the person who introduces cotton manufacture gain?

    A. credit for inventing the machinery

    B. credit for bringing it to the United States

    C. wealth

    D. fame

Discovering Our Past: A History of the United States   103

Copyright © McGraw-Hill Education. Permission is granted to reproduce for classroom use.

> "If we look to the history of other nations, ancient or modern, we find no example of growth so rapid—so gigantic; of a people so prosperous and happy. In [thinking about] what we still have to perform, the heart of every citizen must expand with joy when he reflects how near our Government has approached to perfection."
>
> —from James Monroe's Inaugural Address, March 1817

_____ **13.** As summed up in this quote by President James Monroe, in the years following the War of 1812 Americans had a new spirit of

     A. national pride.   **C.** hard work.

     B. perfection.   **D.** respecting ancient cultures.

_____ **14.** In the passage, what does Monroe say should give American citizens joy?

     A. how large the country has grown

     B. how nearly perfect the government is

     C. the study of history

     D. the tasks still to be done

_____ **15.** What was available in New England that was needed to run factory machinery?

     A. cloth   **C.** ports

     B. farm equipment   **D.** waterpower

_____ **16.** Economic freedom, profit, private property, and competition are the major elements of which type of economic system?

     A. businesses

     B. corporation

     C. free enterprise

     D. industrial growth

_____ **17.** How did business and government officials plan to connect New York City with the Great Lakes Region?

     A. by building a canal

     B. by building a steamboat

     C. by building the National Road

     D. by building the Wilderness Road

_____ **18.** What was the purpose of Henry Clay's American System?

    A. to help the economy in each section of the country

    B. to keep an even balance of power in the Senate

    C. to pass the Tariff of 1816

    D. to take away money for internal improvements

_____ **19.** When Spanish officials realized that they could not hold Florida against the Americans, what did they do?

    A. They agreed to cede Florida to the United States.

    B. They attacked St. Marks and Pensacola.

    C. They gained more power in South America.

    D. They issued a statement warning other nations to stay out of Florida.

_____ **20.** In three decisions in the early 1800s, whose powers were backed by the Supreme Court?

    A. the government of the states

    B. the federal government

    C. the state of Maryland

    D. the state of New York

DIRECTIONS: Short Answer Answer each of the following questions.

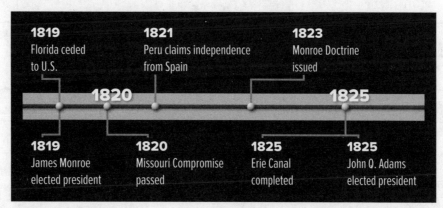

21. Study the time line. Under whose presidential administration was the Missouri Compromise passed?

_____

Chapter 11 Test, Traditional *cont.*

network

Growth and Expansion

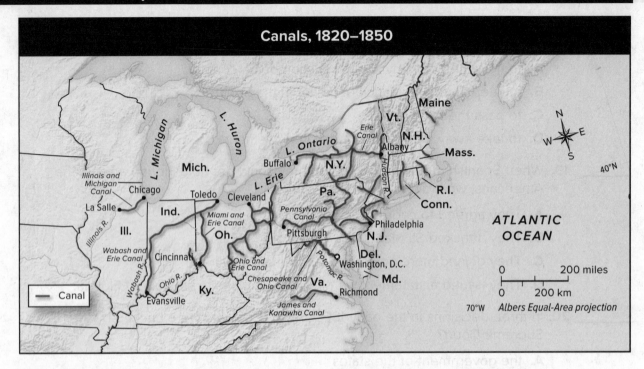

Canals, 1820–1850

22. According to the map, which of the five Great Lakes had the most canals connected to it in 1850?

_____

_____

_____

23. Why did many cities develop along rivers?

_____

_____

_____

24. What was the purpose of the Monroe Doctrine?

_____

_____

_____

DIRECTIONS: Essay Answer the following question on a separate piece of paper.

25. Why did the Industrial Revolution in the United States begin in New England?

Chapter 11 Test, Document-Based Questions

networks

Growth and Expansion

DIRECTIONS: Short Answer Answer each of the following questions.

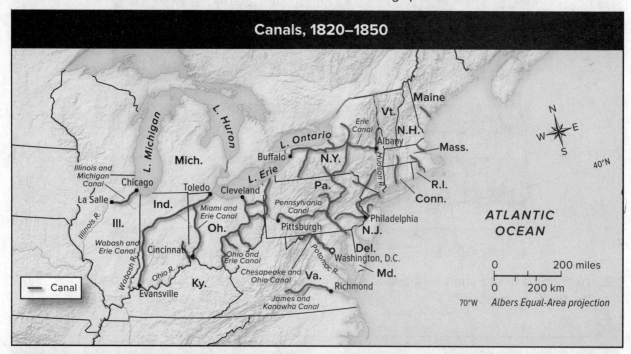

Canals, 1820–1850

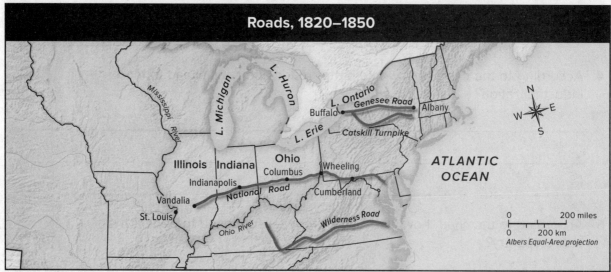

Roads, 1820–1850

1. According to the two maps, which road most nearly followed the route of the Erie Canal?

_____

2. According to the second map, the National Road ends in Vandalia, Illinois. Why do you think Ohio asked the government to build this road?

_____

Henry Clay's American System

The policy would have enforced a protective tariff to get funding for transportation improvements.

↓

These improvements would be the construction of better roads and canals.

↓

This would allow industrialization to prosper because the raw materials of the South and the West could easily and inexpensively get to the North and the East to be manufactured.

↓

The manufactured goods could then be shipped back out to the South and the West.

3. According to the chart, what were the two improvements that Clay intended his tariffs to support?

_____

_____

_____

4. According to the chart, how would better roads and canals lead to more industrialization?

_____

_____

_____

5. According to the chart, how was Clay's proposal supposed to benefit the entire country?

_____

_____

_____

DIRECTIONS: Essay Answer the following question on a separate piece of paper.

6. Explain how advances in technology and transportation in New England were influenced by geography of the United States.

Lesson Quiz 12-1

networks

The Jackson Era

DIRECTIONS: Matching Match each item with the correct statement below.

_____ **1.** increased the prices of European goods

A. Andrew Jackson

_____ **2.** majority

B. John Quincy Adams

_____ **3.** plurality

C. largest single share

_____ **4.** nicknamed "Old Hickory"

D. more than half

_____ **5.** supported the creation of a national bank

E. tariff

DIRECTIONS: Multiple Choice Indicate the answer choice that best completes the statement or answers the question.

_____ **6.** Presidential candidates who receive the backing of their home states rather than that of the national party are called

    A. "favorite son" candidates.

    B. "home state" candidates.

    C. "national party" candidates.

    D. "state party" candidates.

_____ **7.** Introduced in the 1828 presidential election, what became a permanent part of American political life?

    A. campaign contributions   **C.** plurality

    B. mudslinging   **D.** political cartoons

_____ **8.** Andrew Jackson's supporters replaced caucuses with

    A. delegate conventions.   **C.** selection meetings.

    B. nominating conventions.   **D.** state conventions.

_____ **9.** The only Americans allowed to vote in 1824 and 1828 were

    A. white men.

    B. white men who owned land.

    C. white men and women.

    D. white women.

_____ **10.** Which law was intended to allow the president to use the United States military to enforce federal law?

    A. Congressional Act   **C.** Military Bill

    B. Force Bill   **D.** Presidential Act

Lesson Quiz 12-2

netw⊚rks

The Jackson Era

DIRECTIONS: Completion Enter the appropriate word(s) to complete the statement.

1. In 1830 President _____ pushed the Indian Removal Act through Congress.

2. In 1834 Congress set aside an area for Native Americans, most of it in what is today the state of _____.

3. President Jackson ignored the Supreme Court's decision in the case of
_____.

4. The "Trail Where They Cried" is also called the "Trail of _____."

5. The "Black Seminoles" were actually _____.

DIRECTIONS: Multiple Choice Indicate the answer choice that best completes the statement or answers the question.

_____ 6. Which act allowed the federal government to pay Native Americans to move west?

   A. Federal Act   **C.** Native American Act

   B. Indian Removal Act   **D.** Settlers Act

_____ 7. In which Supreme Court decision did Chief Justice John Marshall rule that Georgia had no right to interfere with the Cherokee?

   A. *Jackson* v. *Georgia*   **C.** *McCulloch* v. *Maryland*

   B. *Marbury* v. *Madison*   **D.** *Worcester* v. *Georgia*

_____ 8. Who were the only Native Americans who successfully resisted their removal?

   A. Cherokee   **C.** Sauk

   B. Fox   **D.** Seminole

_____ 9. The Cherokee, Creek, Seminole, Chickasaw, and Choctaw peoples were collectively known as

   A. the "Five Civilized Tribes."   **C.** the "Native American Nation."

   B. the "Five Warrior Tribes."   **D.** the "Native American People."

_____ 10. Which of these prompted calls for additional troops to fight the Seminole in Florida?

   A. Black Seminole Massacre   **C.** Miami Massacre

   B. Dade Massacre   **D.** Tallahassee Massacre

Lesson Quiz 12-3

The Jackson Era

networks

DIRECTIONS: True/False Indicate whether the statement is true or false.

_____ **1.** Nicholas Biddle, president of the Second Bank of America, came from a wealthy family.

_____ **2.** Andrew Jackson was reelected president in 1832.

_____ **3.** Van Buren's *laissez-faire* economic approach ended the Panic of 1837.

_____ **4.** The Whigs' campaign slogan for the 1840 election was "Tippecanoe and Tyler Too."

_____ **5.** William Henry Harrison served two terms as president.

DIRECTIONS: Multiple Choice Indicate the answer choice that best completes the statement or answers the question.

_____ **6.** Which issue did Henry Clay and Daniel Webster use to try to defeat Andrew Jackson in the 1832 presidential election?

 A. Bank of the United States

 B. Congressional annual salaries

 C. Jackson's place of birth

 D. veto power for the president

_____ **7.** President Jackson believed the Bank of the United States

 A. should be supported at all costs.

 B. unfairly favored poor people.

 C. unfairly favored wealthy people.

 D. was corrupt.

_____ **8.** Two months after President Martin Van Buren took office, the United States entered in

 A. a severe depression.

 B. a light recession.

 C. an international profit trade era.

 D. a prosperity era.

_____ **9.** Which symbol did the Whigs adopt for themselves during the 1840 election?

 A. a bank **C.** a log cabin

 B. a donkey **D.** an elephant

Chapter 12 Test, Traditional

netw⊙rks

The Jackson Era

DIRECTIONS: True/False Indicate whether the statement is true or false.

_____ **1.** John Quincy Adams was the son of earlier president John Adams.

_____ **2.** In 1828 Andrew Jackson was selected as the Republican presidential candidate.

_____ **3.** Andrew Jackson was born into a wealthy family.

_____ **4.** Once he became president, Jackson fired many federal employees and replaced them with his supporters.

_____ **5.** John C. Calhoun believed individual states had the right to nullify federal laws.

DIRECTIONS: Matching Match each item with the correct statement below.

_____ **6.** name given to an alleged deal between Clay and Adams in the 1824 election

_____ **7.** favored states' rights in the 1828 election

_____ **8.** a system where appointed officials, not elected ones, carry out laws

_____ **9.** political party that wanted a strong central government in 1828

_____ **10.** an attempt to ruin a candidate's personal reputation

A. bureaucracy

B. Democrats

C. mudslinging

D. Republicans

E. the "corrupt bargain"

DIRECTIONS: Multiple Choice Indicate the answer choice that best completes the statement or answers the question.

_____ **11.** Which group decided the 1824 United States presidential election?

    A. the Electoral College

    B. the House of Representatives

    C. the popular vote

    D. the vice president

_____ **12.** Which case determined that the existence of the Second Bank of the United States was constitutional?

    A. *Cherokee Nation* v. *Georgia*

    B. *Jackson* v. *Oklahoma*

    C. *McCulloch* v. *Maryland*

    D. *Worcester* v. *Georgia*

_____ **13.** Which act did Congress pass to force the relocation of Native Americans?

    A. the Alien Act   **C.** the Naturalization Act

    B. the Indian Removal Act   **D.** the Relocation Act

_____ **14.** What did the U.S. government use as a justification for relocating the Cherokee people?

    A. the Treaty of Georgia

    B. the Treaty of Moultrie Creek

    C. the Treaty of New Echota

    D. the Treaty of Worcester

_____ **15.** The Seminole people successfully resisted their removal from which state?

    A. Alabama   **C.** Georgia

    B. Florida   **D.** South Carolina

_____ **16.** Which president persuaded Congress to create an independent national treasury in 1840?

    A. Clay   **C.** Van Buren

    B. Jackson   **D.** Webster

_____ **17.** Winning candidates who give government jobs to their supporters are making use of which of the following?

    A. *laissez-faire*

    B. Executive Privilege

    C. the Electoral College

    D. the spoils system

> "[This election is a contest] between an honest patriotism, . . . on the one side, and an unholy, selfish ambition, . . . on the other."
>
> —from a convention resolution of Republicans, Saratoga County, New York

_____ **18.** These words, placed on a handbill during the 1828 presidential campaign, are an example of

    A. bureaucracy.

    B. mudslinging.

    C. rumors.

    D. the spoils system.

DIRECTIONS: Short Answer Answer the following questions on a separate piece of paper.

Democrats	Republicans
• represented the South and the West	• represented the North and the East
• consisted largely of immigrants and big-city laborers	• consisted largely of merchants and wealthy farmers
• supported tariffs only to raise revenue	• supported tariffs to protect U.S. trade
• supported states' rights	• supported a strong central government
• supported an independent treasury	• supported a government bank

19. According to the chart, when the Democratic-Republicans split into two separate parties, where did most Republicans live?

20. According to the chart, on which major issues did the two parties agree?

21. According to the chart, which party feared the idea of the federal government passing unconstitutional laws?

22. According to the chart, what party would most industrial workers in Chicago support?

Chapter 12 Test, Traditional *cont.*

networks

The Jackson Era

DIRECTIONS: Essay Answer the following question.

23. What was the "corrupt bargain" between Henry Clay and John Quincy Adams?

_____

_____

_____

_____

_____

_____

_____

_____

_____

Discovering Our Past: A History of the United States

Chapter 12 Test, Document-Based Questions   netw⊙rks

The Jackson Era

DIRECTIONS: Multiple Choice Indicate the answer choice that best completes the statement or answers the question.

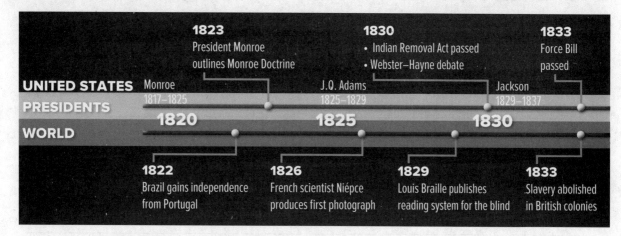

_____ **1.** During which administration was the Indian Removal Act passed?

   A. Harrison

   B. Jackson

   C. J.Q. Adams

   D. Monroe

DIRECTIONS: Short Answer Answer each of the following questions.

> "And is it supposed that the wandering savage has a stronger attachment to his home than the settled, civilized Christian? Is it more afflicting to him to leave the graves of his fathers than it is to our brothers and children? Rightly considered, the policy of the general government toward the red man is not only liberal but generous. He is unwilling to submit to the laws of the states and mingle with their population. To save him from this alternative, or perhaps utter annihilation, the general government kindly offers him a new home, and proposes to pay the whole expense of his removal and settlement."
>
> —President Andrew Jackson, to Congress, December 1830

2. Which proposed piece of legislation is Jackson most likely supporting in the above quote?

_____

3. Which single word from the quote best summarizes Jackson's opinion of Native Americans?

_____

Chapter 12 Test, Document-Based
Questions *cont.*

4. How does Jackson describe white settlers?

_____

5. What does Jackson feel Native Americans have done to create the need for the government to relocate them?

_____

_____

6. What does Jackson claim will likely happen to Native Americans if they are not relocated?

_____

_____

7. How does Jackson characterize the government's forced relocation of Native Americans?

_____

_____

DIRECTIONS: Essay Answer the following question.

8. Explain the causes and effects of the Indian Removal Act.

_____

_____

_____

_____

_____

_____

_____

_____

Lesson Quiz 13-1

netw⊚rks

Manifest Destiny

DIRECTIONS: Matching Match each item with the correct statement below.

_____ **1.** missionary

A. mountain man

_____ **2.** lost to James Polk

B. Narcissa Whitman

_____ **3.** American merchant

C. John Jacob Astor

_____ **4.** fur trapper

D. John Quincy Adams

_____ **5.** negotiated a treaty with Spain

E. Henry Clay

DIRECTIONS: Multiple Choice Indicate the answer choice that best completes the statement or answers the question.

_____ **6.** Oregon Country was which direction from California?

A. east

C. south

B. north

D. west

_____ **7.** Which philosophy meant that the United States was meant to extend its boundaries all the way to the Pacific?

A. Emigrant Theory

C. Manifest Destiny

B. Joint Occupation

D. Rendezvous Philosophy

"After Laramie we entered the great American desert, which was hard on the teams. Sickness became common."

—Catherine Sager Pringle, 1844

_____ **8.** As indicated in this quotation, what was a frequent problem that pioneers faced along the Oregon Trail?

A. fatigue

C. illness

B. food shortages

D. Native American attacks

_____ **9.** The main route that settlers took through the Rocky Mountains to Oregon was called the

A. East Pass.

C. South Pass.

B. North Pass.

D. West Pass.

_____ **10.** One reason the United States claimed Oregon Country was because of

A. the 1844 presidential election.

C. the Treaty of Guadalupe.

B. the Lewis and Clark expedition.

D. the Whitman massacre.

Lesson Quiz 13-2

networks

Manifest Destiny

DIRECTIONS: True/False Indicate whether the statement is true or false.

_____ 1. The defenders of the Alamo played an important role in the fight for the independence of Texas.

_____ 2. The territorial capital of Florida was Pensacola.

_____ 3. A significant early battle was fought at the Alamo in San Antonio.

_____ 4. After the Battle of San Jacinto, Santa Anna swore he would keep fighting.

_____ 5. After being elected president of Texas, Juan Seguín sent a delegation to Washington.

DIRECTIONS: Multiple Choice Indicate the answer choice that best completes the statement or answers the question.

_____ 6. Which group represented about half of the population of Florida in the 1830s?

    A. enslaved people   **C.** Tejanos

    B. rancheros   **D.** Virginians

_____ 7. Florida could not become a state until which of the following happened?

    A. A free state joined the Union.

    B. A slave state joined the Union.

    C. It agreed to end slavery.

    D. Texas joined the Union.

_____ 8. Who was one of the first Americans to settle in Texas?

    A. Davy Crockett   **C.** Stephen Austin

    B. Jim Bowie   **D.** William Travis

_____ 9. What happened to the Texan forces at the Alamo?

    A. They declared Texas independent.

    B. They negotiated a truce.

    C. They were defeated.

    D. They won a major victory.

_____ 10. Which president refused Texans' request for annexation?

    A. Andrew Jackson   **C.** James Polk

    B. Henry Clay   **D.** Sam Houston

Lesson Quiz 13-3

networks

Manifest Destiny

DIRECTIONS: True/False Indicate whether the statement is true or false.

_____ **1.** At one time, Mexico was claimed by Spain.

_____ **2.** Native Americans were well treated on Mexican ranchos.

_____ **3.** Mexico believed that the Rio Grande formed the Texas-Mexico border.

_____ **4.** As part of the terms of the Treaty of Guadalupe Hidalgo, Mexico received half as much money as the United States had offered before the war began.

_____ **5.** The United States did not attain its goal of capturing Mexico City.

DIRECTIONS: Multiple Choice Indicate the answer choice that best completes the statement or answers the question.

_____ **6.** What did President James K. Polk use as grounds for declaring war against Mexico?

    A. annexation of Texas by Mexico

    B. declaration of the border by Mexico

    C. a Mexican attack on American forces

    D. Mexico's nonpayment of debts

_____ **7.** What was one reason William Becknell's route to Mexico became popular?

    A. It avoided the prairies.

    B. It was guarded by soldiers.

    C. The route was flat and had stops for water.

    D. The route was located on American land.

_____ **8.** What did Junípero Serra do?

    A. explored the West as far as California

    B. founded a chain of missions

    C. invaded Mexico with Zachary Taylor

    D. made a fortune with his trading posts

_____ **9.** What was the final step of President Polk's plan to defeat Mexico?

    A. capture Mexico City

    B. declare California's independence

    C. stop traffic along the Santa Fe Trail

    D. topple Santa Anna

Lesson Quiz 13-4

networks

Manifest Destiny

DIRECTIONS: Completion Enter the appropriate word(s) to complete the statement.

1. Under the Land Law of 1851, many _____ lost their land.

2. As a result of the _____, San Francisco became a boomtown.

3. After the United States acquired Utah, _____ was named governor.

4. Gold was discovered in 1848 at _____ in California.

5. Frontier law was often handled by self-appointed _____.

DIRECTIONS: Multiple Choice Indicate the answer choice that best completes the statement or answers the question.

_____ 6. Which event, beginning in 1849, had long-lasting effects on California's economy?

    A. discovery of gold   **C.** shipping to the North

    B. growth of industry   **D.** trade with Mexico

_____ 7. Discoveries made in California more than doubled the world's supply of which item?

    A. farmland   **C.** oil

    B. gold   **D.** water

_____ 8. What was the largest single migration in American history?

    A. forty-niners to California

    B. Mormons to Utah

    C. mountain men to Oregon

    D. traders to Mexico

_____ 9. Which of the following groups made huge profits during the California Gold Rush?

    A. boomtown merchants   **C.** Mormon traders

    B. forty-niners   **D.** rancheros

_____ 10. What was one of Joseph Smith's basic beliefs?

    A. California should become a state.

    B. Mormons should leave Illinois.

    C. President Polk treated Mexico unfairly.

    D. Property should be held in common.

Chapter 13 Test, Traditional

netw⊙rks

Manifest Destiny

DIRECTIONS: True/False Indicate whether the statement is true or false.

_____ **1.** In the early 1800s, the United States, Great Britain, Mexico, and Russia all laid claim to part of Oregon Country.

_____ **2.** After exhausting the beaver supply in Oregon Country, many mountain men found work as guides.

_____ **3.** In 1844 the Democratic Party's campaign slogan referred to conflict with Great Britain over Oregon Country.

_____ **4.** President Martin Van Buren agreed to annex Texas.

_____ **5.** The Mexican ranchos had Native Americans working the land in exchange for food and shelter.

DIRECTIONS: Matching Match each item with the correct statement below.

_____ **6.** took the law into their own hands   **A.** vigilantes

_____ **7.** route to western lands   **B.** Oregon Trail

_____ **8.** huge Mexican properties   **C.** Sam Houston

_____ **9.** commander of Texan forces   **D.** ranchos

_____ **10.** Mexicans living in California   **E.** Californios

DIRECTIONS: Multiple Choice Indicate the answer choice that best completes the statement or answers the question.

_____ **11.** What was the last country to challenge the United States's control of Oregon?

    A. Britain   **C.** Russia

    B. Mexico   **D.** Spain

_____ **12.** What allowed people from both Britain and the United States to settle in Oregon Country?

    A. joint occupation   **C.** Oregon Country occupation

    B. Manifest Destiny   **D.** rendezvous

_____ **13.** Jim Bridger and Kit Carson lived in the West and worked as

    A. farmers.   **C.** guides.

    B. merchants.   **D.** missionaries.

_____ **14.** Whom did Texas choose as its president after Texas won independence from Mexico?

    A. Davy Crockett

    B. Jim Bowie

    C. Sam Houston

    D. William B. Travis

_____ **15.** Mountain men made their living as

    A. merchants.

    B. missionaries.

    C. surveyors.

    D. trappers.

"We reached the camping place. What first struck our eye was several long rows of Indian tents (lodges), extending along the Green River for at least a mile. Indians and whites were mingled here in varied groups. Of the Indians there had come chiefly Snakes, Flatheads and Nezperces, peaceful tribes, living beyond the Rocky Mountains. Of whites the agents of the different trading companies and a quantity of trappers had found their way here, visiting this fair of the wilderness to buy and to sell, to renew old contracts and to make new ones, to make arrangements for future meetings, to meet old friends, to tell of adventures they had been through, and to spend for once a jolly day."

—Adolph Wislizenus, a German traveler in the West

_____ **16.** Who came to the meeting of mountain men described in the excerpt?

    A. agents of trading companies, settlers, soldiers

    B. Native Americans, agents of trading companies, trappers

    C. settlers, soldiers, trappers, agents of trading companies

    D. trappers, church leaders, Native Americans

_____ **17.** Which of the following best describes the purpose of the meeting as described in the excerpt?

    A. business and pleasure

    B. pleasure and government

    C. business only

    D. government only

Manifest Destiny

> "We are creeping along slowly, one wagon after another, the same old gait, the same thing over, out of one mud hole into another all day."
>
> —Amelia Stewart Knight, 1853

_____ **18.** What emotion does this quotation, from a traveler on the Oregon Trail, show?

A. anger

B. boredom

C. excitement

D. fear

> "[T]he people of Texas, in solemn convention assembled, appealing to a candid world for the necessities of our condition, do hereby resolve and declare that our political connection with the Mexican nation has forever ended; and that the people of Texas do now constitute a free, sovereign, and independent republic."
>
> —March 2, 1836

_____ **19.** This resolution is a quotation from the

A. Florida Declaration of Sovereignty.

B. Houston Proclamation.

C. Mexican Constitution.

D. Texas Declaration of Independence.

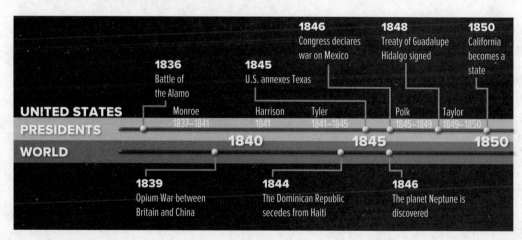

_____ **20.** Under whose presidential administration was the United States at war with Mexico?

A. Harrison

B. Polk

C. Taylor

D. Tyler

Discovering Our Past: A History of the United States

Chapter 13 Test, Traditional *cont.*

Manifest Destiny

DIRECTIONS: Short Answer Answer each of the following questions.

21. Why did President Andrew Jackson refuse Houston's request to annex Texas?

_____

_____

_____

22. Who were the forty-niners and why did they come to California?

_____

_____

23. How did the Gold Rush affect California's population?

_____

_____

24. Why did the Mormons leave New York?

_____

_____

_____

DIRECTIONS: Essay Answer the following question on a separate piece of paper.

25. What was the end result of Mexico's offering land to new settlers in the 1820s?

Discovering Our Past: A History of the United States

Chapter 13 Test, Document-Based Questions

networks

Manifest Destiny

DIRECTIONS: Short Answer Answer each of the following questions.

Election of 1844

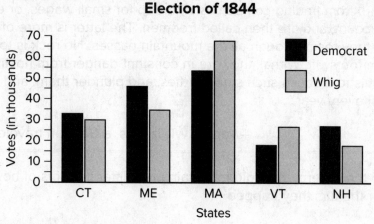

Source: Presidential Election Returns, 1792–1972

1. Which of these states did the Democratic candidate James K. Polk win in the 1844 presidential election?

_____

_____

_____

_____

2. Which candidate won more states, the Whig candidate Henry Clay or the Democrat candidate James Polk?

_____

_____

_____

_____

3. In which state were the most votes won by either candidate? Approximately how many votes were won by each candidate?

_____

_____

_____

_____

Chapter 13 Test, Document-Based Questions *cont.*

networks

Manifest Destiny

> "[Mountain men] either receive their outfit, consisting of horses, beaver traps, a gun, powder and lead, from trading companies, and trap for small wages, or else they act on their own account, and are then called freemen. The latter is more often the case. In small parties they roam through all the mountain passes. No rock is too steep for them; no stream too swift. Withal, they are in constant danger from hostile Indians, whose delight it is to ambush such small parties, and plunder them, and scalp them. Such victims fall every year."
>
> —Adolph Wislizenus, a German traveler in the West

4. According to the excerpt, how did mountain men differ in terms of how they were paid for the furs they trapped?

_____

_____

_____

_____

5. According to the excerpt, what challenges did mountain men face?

_____

_____

_____

_____

6. According to the excerpt, what characteristics do mountain men have?

_____

_____

_____

_____

Discovering Our Past: A History of the United States

Lesson Quiz 14-1

netw⊙rks

North and South

DIRECTIONS: True/False Indicate whether the statement is true or false.

_____ **1.** The steamboat, the steam-powered locomotive, the sewing machine, the telegraph, and the steel-tipped plow were some of the major innovations of the 1800s.

_____ **2.** The sewing machine increased the rate at which clothing was produced.

_____ **3.** Wider and deeper canals allowed steamboats to travel on major rivers.

_____ **4.** Clipper ships could sail at speeds of up to 300 miles per hour.

_____ **5.** After the invention of revolutionary farming methods, settlers left the Great Plains area.

DIRECTIONS: Multiple Choice Indicate the answer choice that best completes the statement or answers the question.

_____ **6.** By 1860 where were most of the country's goods manufactured?

    A. Northeast   **C.** Southeast

    B. Northwest   **D.** Southwest

_____ **7.** By 1860 the United States had almost 31,000

    A. canals.   **C.** miles of railroad tracks.

    B. clipper ships.   **D.** miles of telegraph lines.

_____ **8.** Which invention filled the need for a method of communication that kept up with industrial growth and fast-paced travel?

    A. mechanical reaper   **C.** steam engine

    B. railroads   **D.** telegraph

_____ **9.** What did John Deere invent in 1837?

    A. Morse code   **C.** steel-tipped plow

    B. clipper ship   **D.** telegraph

_____ **10.** Which invention ensured that raising wheat would remain the main economic activity in the Midwestern prairies?

    A. mechanical horse

    B. mechanical reaper

    C. steel thresher

    D. steel-tipped plow

Discovering Our Past: A History of the United States

Lesson Quiz 14-2

networks

North and South

DIRECTIONS: Matching Match each item with the correct statement below.

_____ **1.** a refusal to work

_____ **2.** unfair opinion not based on fact

_____ **3.** became a licensed lawyer

_____ **4.** founded Lowell Female Labor Reform Organization

_____ **5.** formed by nativists in 1849

A. strike

B. Know-Nothing Party

C. Macon B. Allen

D. prejudice

E. Sarah G. Bagley

DIRECTIONS: Multiple Choice Indicate the answer choice that best completes the statement or answers the question.

_____ **6.** What did workers do to improve their working conditions?

    A. created factories

    B. formed trade unions

    C. scheduled breaks

    D. survived famines

_____ **7.** What problem did women face in the workplace?

    A. discrimination   **C.** literacy

    B. innovation   **D.** promotion

_____ **8.** What caused the increase in Irish migration to the United States?

    A. famine   **C.** labor unions

    B. free land   **D.** prejudice

_____ **9.** From which country did the second largest group of immigrants arrive into the United States between 1820 and 1860?

    A. Ireland

    B. Germany

    C. Great Britain

    D. Mexico

_____ **10.** What were people called who were opposed to immigration?

    A. anti-aliens

    B. overseers

    C. nativists

    D. yeomen

Lesson Quiz 14-3

networks

North and South

DIRECTIONS: Completion Enter the appropriate word(s) to complete the statement.

1. By 1850 the institution of _____ was growing stronger than ever in the South.

2. Many in the South preferred an agricultural economy and did not want _____.

3. The cotton gin could clean cotton _____ faster than a worker.

4. Most Southerners had their money invested in enslaved African Americans and _____.

5. In 1860 the economy of the _____ was dependent on cotton.

DIRECTIONS: Multiple Choice Indicate the answer choice that best completes the statement or answers the question.

_____ 6. Which of the following kept the price of cotton high in the years before 1860?

    A. cotton gin   **C.** large plantations

    B. demand in Europe   **D.** slavery

_____ 7. Which area became a center for the sale and transport of enslaved people throughout the South?

    A. Deep South   **C.** Upper South

    B. Northeast   **D.** West

_____ 8. What was the main crop of the Deep South?

    A. cotton   **C.** sugarcane

    B. rice   **D.** tobacco

_____ 9. In general, what did farmers and factory owners in the South use to transport their goods?

    A. canals

    B. horse-drawn carts

    C. natural waterways

    D. railroads

_____ 10. Which South Carolina merchant opened a textile factory?

    A. Eyre Crowe

    B. Eli Whitney

    C. Joseph Reid Anderson

    D. William Gregg

Lesson Quiz 14-4

networks

North and South

DIRECTIONS: Matching Match each item with its definition.

_____ 1. ability to read and write

_____ 2. farmed landlords' estates

_____ 3. brief

_____ 4. to purchase goods with loaned money

_____ 5. permitted by law

A. credit

B. legal

C. literacy

D. short in duration

E. tenant farmers

DIRECTIONS: Multiple Choice Indicate the answer choice that best completes the statement or answers the question.

_____ 6. The largest group of whites in the South was made up of

    A. plantation owners.
    B. rural poor.
    C. tenant farmers.
    D. yeomen.

_____ 7. The main goal of large plantation owners was to

    A. build factories.
    B. produce more cotton.
    C. earn a profit.
    D. build a larger plantation.

_____ 8. Who was the religious leader who led a slave revolt in 1831?

    A. Eli Whitney
    B. Frederick Douglass
    C. Harriet Tubman
    D. Nat Turner

_____ 9. African American folk songs that expressed the passionate beliefs of the South's enslaved people were called

    A. overseers.
    B. slave codes.
    C. spirituals.
    D. yeomen.

_____ 10. The network of safe houses that assisted runaway enslaved people was known as

    A. the runaway homes.
    B. the secret passage.
    C. the slave code.
    D. the Underground Railroad.

Discovering Our Past: A History of the United States

Chapter 14 Test, Traditional

network

North and South

DIRECTIONS: True/False Indicate whether the statement is true or false.

_____ **1.** After industrialization, workers' tasks changed.

_____ **2.** After her own escape from slavery, Harriet Tubman returned to the South many times, helping many enslaved African Americans escape to freedom in the North.

_____ **3.** Plantation owners with many enslaved workers were considered very wealthy.

_____ **4.** Immigrants quickly forgot their customs and language.

_____ **5.** The telegraph was invented before the steam-powered locomotive.

DIRECTIONS: Matching Match each item with its definition.

_____ **6.** group of workers with the same skill   **A.** capital

_____ **7.** to purchase goods with loaned money   **B.** credit

_____ **8.** money to invest   **C.** literacy

_____ **9.** unfair treatment of a specific group   **D.** discrimination

_____ **10.** the ability to read and write   **E.** trade union

DIRECTIONS: Multiple Choice Indicate the answer choice that best completes the statement or answers the question.

_____ **11.** In which state did the Great Train Wreck of 1856 occur?

    A. Indiana

    B. Ohio

    C. Pennsylvania

    D. Virginia

_____ **12.** During the 1830s and 1840s, what were people called who were opposed to immigration?

    A. abolitionists

    B. nativists

    C. reservists

    D. yeomen

_____ **13.** Enslaved people expressed their beliefs in religious folk songs called

    A. hymns.   **C.** slave codes.

    B. psalms.   **D.** spirituals.

_____ **14.** What was one of the consequences of the cotton gin?

    A. Deep South farmers grew more wheat.

    B. Domestic slave trade increased.

    C. Plantations hired more tenant farmers.

    D. Southern factories quickly developed.

RAILROADS IN THE NORTH AND SOUTH

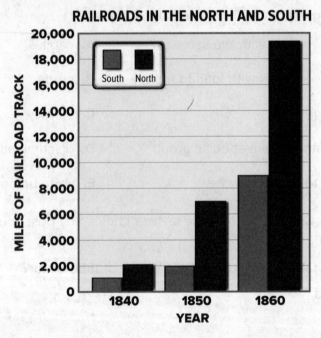

_____ **15.** Based on the graph, which of the following statements is correct?

    A. In 1840 there were more miles of railroad track in the South than in the North.

    B. In 1850 the South more than tripled the miles of tracks it had in 1840.

    C. In 1860 the amount of tracks in both the North and the South had not increased.

    D. In all three decades, the North had more miles of tracks than the South.

_____ **16.** Based on the graph, how many miles of railroad tracks did the North have in 1850?

    A. 200   **C.** 2,000

    B. 700   **D.** 7,000

Chapter 14 Test, Traditional *cont.*

networ⊙rks

_____ 17. By 1840 what was the average workday for factory workers?

    A. 6.7 hours

    B. 8.0 hours

    C. 11.4 hours

    D. 16.2 hours

URBAN AND RURAL POPULATION, 1830–1860

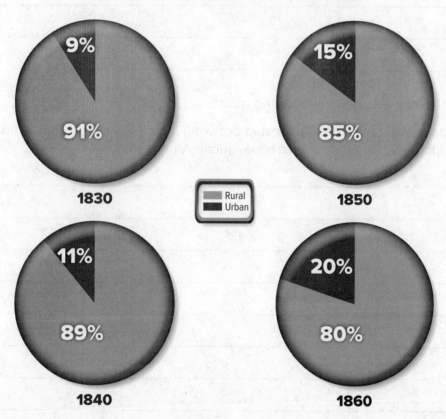

_____ 18. According to the circle graphs, how much did the percentage of people living in urban areas increase from 1830 to 1860?

    A. 9 percent

    B. 11 percent

    C. 15 percent

    D. 20 percent

_____ 19. According to the circle graphs, what percentage of the population lived in urban areas in the year 1850?

    A. 9 percent   **C.** 15 percent

    B. 11 percent   **D.** 85 percent

Discovering Our Past: A History of the United States

Chapter 14 Test, Traditional *cont.*

netw⊕rks

North and South

DIRECTIONS: Short Answer Answer each of the following questions.

20. What did long workdays and dangerous conditions within factories often lead to?

_____

_____

21. What were some reasons for the South's low literacy rate?

_____

_____

_____

DIRECTIONS: Essay Answer the following question.

22. In the South, what was the relationship between increased cotton production and the increased number of enslaved African Americans?

_____

_____

_____

_____

_____

_____

_____

_____

_____

_____

_____

Chapter 14 Test, Document-Based Questions

networks

North and South

DIRECTIONS: Short Answer Answer each of the following questions.

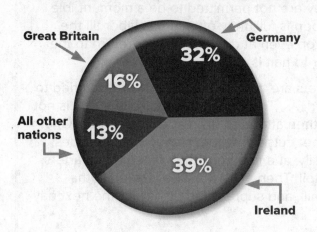

SOURCES OF U.S. IMMIGRATION 1841–1860

Great Britain

Germany

32%

16%

All other nations

13%

39%

Ireland

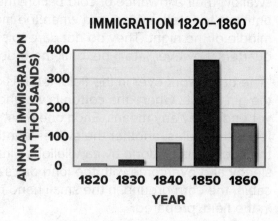

IMMIGRATION 1820–1860

ANNUAL IMMIGRATION (IN THOUSANDS)

400
300
200
100
0

1820 1830 1840 1850 1860

YEAR

1. Based on the information in the graphs, in which year was immigration to the United States the highest?

_____

2. Based on the information in the graphs, what is the percentage of immigrants who came from Great Britain during the period 1841–1860?

_____

3. Based on the information in the graphs, the largest percentage of immigrants came from which nation during the period 1841–1860?

_____

"The hands are required to be in the cotton field as soon as it is light in the morning, and, with the exception of ten or fifteen minutes, which is given them at noon to swallow their allowance of cold bacon, they are not permitted to be a moment idle until it is too dark to see, and when the moon is full, they often times labor till the middle of the night. They do not dare to stop even at dinner time, nor return to the quarters, however late it be, until the order to halt is given by the driver.

"The day's work over in the field, the baskets are 'toted,' or in other words, carried to the gin-house, where the cotton is weighed. . . . This done, the labor of the day is not yet ended, by any means. Each one must then attend to his respective chores. One feeds the mules, another the swine—another cuts the wood, and so forth; besides, the packing is all done by candlelight. Finally, at a late hour, they reach the quarters, sleepy and overcome with the long day's toil. Then a fire must be kindled in the cabin, the corn ground in the small hand-mill, and supper, and dinner for the next day in the field, prepared."

—Solomon Northup, *Twelve Years a Slave*, 1853

4. Which aspect of cotton picking on plantations does this excerpt emphasize?

_____

_____

5. According to the excerpt, how long is a field hand's workday?

_____

6. Explain the meaning of the passage "they are not permitted to be a moment idle until it is too dark to see."

_____

_____

_____

DIRECTIONS: Essay Answer the following question on a separate piece of paper.

7. Why did industry develop more slowly in the South than it did in the North?

Lesson Quiz 15-1

networks

The Spirit of Reform

DIRECTIONS: True/False Indicate whether the statement is true or false.

_____ **1.** A utopia is a community based on a vision of a perfect society.

_____ **2.** Religious leaders fought for the freedom to drink alcohol.

_____ **3.** In 1839 Massachusetts founded the first state-supported school to train teachers.

_____ **4.** Most parents in the 1800s wanted their daughters to be educated and have careers.

_____ **5.** During the 1820s, American artists developed their own style and explored American themes.

DIRECTIONS: Multiple Choice Indicate the answer choice that best completes the statement or answers the question.

_____ **6.** Who opened Hartford School for the Deaf in Connecticut in 1817?

    A. Dorothea Dix   **C.** Samuel Gridley Howe

    B. Horace Mann   **D.** Thomas Gallaudet

_____ **7.** Which was the first college in the United States to admit women and African Americans?

    A. Ashmun Institute   **C.** Mount Holyoke

    B. Harvard University   **D.** Oberlin College of Ohio

_____ **8.** Who was the schoolteacher who helped educate the public about the poor living conditions of the mentally ill?

    A. Dorothea Dix   **C.** George Catlin

    B. Samuel Gridley Howe   **D.** Thomas Gallaudet

_____ **9.** What were people called who stressed the relationship between humans and nature and the importance of the individual conscience?

    A. conscience-raisers   **C.** reformers

    B. naturalists   **D.** transcendentalists

_____ **10.** Which author wrote *Leaves of Grass*?

    A. Emily Dickinson   **C.** Ralph Waldo Emerson

    B. Herman Melville   **D.** Walt Whitman

Lesson Quiz 15-2

networks

The Spirit of Reform

DIRECTIONS: True/False Indicate whether the statement is true or false.

_____ **1.** The American Colonization Society successfully ended slavery.

_____ **2.** William Lloyd Garrison was a spokesperson for immediate emancipation.

_____ **3.** The Grimké sisters grew up in a slaveholding family but became strong opponents of slavery.

_____ **4.** The Underground Railroad carried food to poor areas in the South.

_____ **5.** Opposition to abolitionism sometimes erupted into violence.

DIRECTIONS: Multiple Choice Indicate the answer choice that best completes the statement or answers the question.

_____ **6.** Which definition best fits the word *abolition*?

    A. writing about personal feelings

    B. describing the westward movement

    C. ending discrimination against women

    D. ending slavery

_____ **7.** Which abolitionist was shot and killed by angry whites while escaping his burning newspaper office?

    A. David Walker

    B. Elijah Lovejoy

    C. Harriet Beecher Stowe

    D. William Lloyd Garrison

_____ **8.** How did most African Americans live in the North?

    A. in poverty on farms

    B. in poverty in the cities

    C. moderately wealthily in cities

    D. moderately wealthily on farms

_____ **9.** What did the Grimké sisters do?

    A. founded the American Colonization Society

    B. were leaders in the Quaker religion

    C. spoke out against slavery

    D. started an abolitionist newspaper

Discovering Our Past: A History of the United States

Lesson Quiz 15-3

netw⊙rks

The Spirit of Reform

DIRECTIONS: Multiple Choice Indicate the answer choice that best completes the statement or answers the question.

_____ 1. Who was the woman active in movements promoting suffrage, equal pay, and abolition?

    A. Elizabeth Stanton   **C.** Lucy Stone

    B. Lucretia Mott   **D.** Susan B. Anthony

_____ 2. Maria Mitchell made contributions in which field?

    A. astronomy   **C.** literature

    B. education   **D.** medicine

_____ 3. Who helped to organize the Seneca Falls Convention?

    A. Amelia Jenks Bloomer   **C.** Mary Lyon

    B. Elizabeth Cady Stanton   **D.** Susan B. Anthony

_____ 4. Which was the first state to allow women to divorce their husbands if their husbands had an alcohol problem?

    A. California   **C.** Mississippi

    B. Indiana   **D.** New York

_____ 5. Mount Holyoke was a school for

    A. women.   **C.** ministers.

    B. lawyers.   **D.** astronomers.

DIRECTIONS: Short Answer Answer each of the following questions.

6. What is the meaning of *suffrage*?

_____

7. Which document was issued by the Seneca Falls Convention?

_____

8. Which women's rights leader called for coeducation?

_____

9. Which school did Mary Lyon establish in 1837?

_____

10. Which state was the first to grant women suffrage in 1890?

_____

Chapter 15 Test, Traditional

netw⊙rks

The Spirit of Reform

DIRECTIONS: True/False Indicate whether the statement is true or false.

_____ **1.** The Shakers were the only religious group able to establish a lasting utopian community.

_____ **2.** The abolitionist Sojourner Truth was given her name by her former slaveholder.

_____ **3.** Elizabeth Blackwell graduated first in her medical school class after having been turned down by several other schools.

_____ **4.** In the 1840s students learned to become teachers at normal schools.

_____ **5.** The Grimké sisters spoke out against abolition.

DIRECTIONS: Matching Match each item with the correct statement below.

_____ **6.** abolitionist newspaper   **A.** *Uncle Tom's Cabin*

_____ **7.** book portraying the cruelties of slavery   **B.** Horace Mann

_____ **8.** religious camp meetings   **C.** *The Liberator*

_____ **9.** leader of educational reform   **D.** Walt Whitman

_____ **10.** poet   **E.** revivals

DIRECTIONS: Multiple Choice Indicate the answer choice that best completes the statement or answers the question.

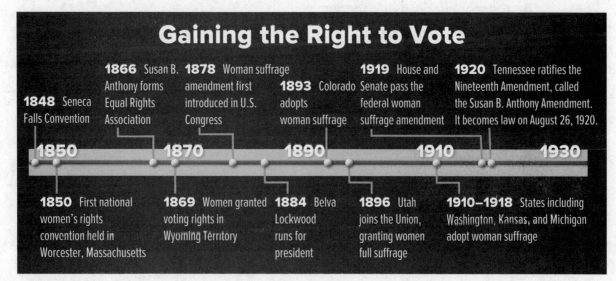

Gaining the Right to Vote

1848 Seneca Falls Convention

1866 Susan B. Anthony forms Equal Rights Association

1878 Woman suffrage amendment first introduced in U.S. Congress

1893 Colorado adopts woman suffrage

1919 House and Senate pass the federal woman suffrage amendment

1920 Tennessee ratifies the Nineteenth Amendment, called the Susan B. Anthony Amendment. It becomes law on August 26, 1920.

1850   **1870**   **1890**   **1910**   **1930**

1850 First national women's rights convention held in Worcester, Massachusetts

1869 Women granted voting rights in Wyoming Territory

1884 Belva Lockwood runs for president

1896 Utah joins the Union, granting women full suffrage

1910–1918 States including Washington, Kansas, and Michigan adopt woman suffrage

_____ **11.** Based on the time line on the previous page, in which year were women granted voting rights in Wyoming Territory?

  A. 1869

  B. 1878

  C. 1893

  D. 1919

_____ **12.** Based on the time line on the previous page, which three states adopted woman suffrage in 1910–1918?

  A. Colorado, Wyoming, Utah

  B. Colorado, Utah, Kansas

  C. Washington, Michigan, Kansas

  D. Washington, Kansas, Tennessee

_____ **13.** By 1830 what was the most pressing social issue for reformers?

  A. antislavery movement

  B. free education

  C. prohibition

  D. women's right to vote

_____ **14.** Samuel Cornish and John Russwurm started *Freedom's Journal,* the country's first

  A. African American newspaper.

  B. antislavery publication.

  C. pro-slavery newspaper.

  D. spiritual review.

_____ **15.** Which famous African American abolitionist, speaker, and writer escaped from slavery as a runaway?

  A. John Russwurm

  B. Frederick Douglass

  C. Samuel Cornish

  D. William Lloyd Garrison

_____ **16.** Who was the most famous conductor of the Underground Railroad?

    A. Frederick Douglass

    B. Harriet Tubman

    C. Sojourner Truth

    D. William Lloyd Garrison

_____ **17.** In 1830 free African American leaders held an antislavery convention in which city?

    A. Baltimore

    B. Chicago

    C. New York City

    D. Philadelphia

_____ **18.** Writers Margaret Fuller and Ralph Waldo Emerson were

    A. enslaved people.

    B. utopians.

    C. revivalists.

    D. transcendentalists.

_____ **19.** Abolitionists like Lucretia Mott helped organize the

    A. education movement.

    B. gradualism movement.

    C. temperance movement.

    D. women's rights movement.

> "Under a government which imprisons any unjustly, the true place for a just man is also a prison."

_____ **20.** Read the quotation above. Which of the following people authored the quote and was a transcendentalist who was jailed for not paying a tax that would support war?

    A. Dorothea Dix

    B. Emily Dickinson

    C. Henry David Thoreau

    D. Ralph Waldo Emerson

Chapter 15 Test, Traditional *cont.*

The Spirit of Reform

DIRECTIONS: Short Answer Answer each of the following questions.

21. What was the wave of religious fervor that stirred the nation to reform in the early 1800s?

_____

22. Which group of people with special needs did Samuel Howe help?

_____

> "I looked at my hands to see if I was the same person now that I was free. . . . I felt like I was in heaven."
>
> —Harriet Tubman, on her escape from slavery, 1849

23. In this quotation, why does Tubman look at her hands?

_____

_____

> "Oh, Woman! from thy happy hearth,
>
> Extend thy gentle hand to save
>
> The poor and perishing of earth—
>
> The chained and stricken slave!"
>
> —John Greenleaf Whittier

24. What do these lines from a poem indicate about Whittier's feelings?

_____

_____

DIRECTIONS: Essay Answer the following question on a separate piece of paper.

25. Compare and contrast the goals of the women's movement and the antislavery movement in the 1800s. In what ways were the two movements linked?

Chapter 15 Test, Document-Based Questions

netw⊛rks

The Spirit of Reform

DIRECTIONS: Short Answer Answer each of the following questions.

> "I am aware, that many object to the severity of my language; but is there not cause for severity? I will be as harsh as truth, and as uncompromising as justice. On this subject, I do not wish to think, or speak, or write, with moderation. No! no! Tell a man whose house is on fire to give a moderate alarm. . . . [U]rge me not to use moderation in a cause like the present. I am in earnest—I will not equivocate—I will not excuse—I will not retreat a single inch—AND I WILL BE HEARD."
>
> —William Lloyd Garrison, *The Liberator*, 1831

1. What issue is Garrison describing in this excerpt?

_____

_____

2. How did many white people react to Garrison's views on slavery?

_____

_____

> "What, to the American slave, is your Fourth of July? . . . To him, your celebration is a sham; your boasted liberty, an unholy license; your national greatness, swelling vanity; your sounds of rejoicing are empty and heartless; your denunciation of tyrants, brass-fronted impudence; your shouts of liberty and equality, hollow mockery; your prayers and hymns, your sermons and thanksgivings, with all your religious parade and solemnity, are, to Him, mere bombast, fraud, deception, impiety, and hypocrisy—a thin veil to cover up crimes which would disgrace a nation of savages. There is not a nation on the earth guilty of practices more shocking and bloody than are the people of the United States, at this very hour."
>
> —Frederick Douglass, Independence Day speech, Rochester, New York, 1841

3. Why does Douglass say that the Fourth of July celebration is a "sham" to enslaved people?

_____

_____

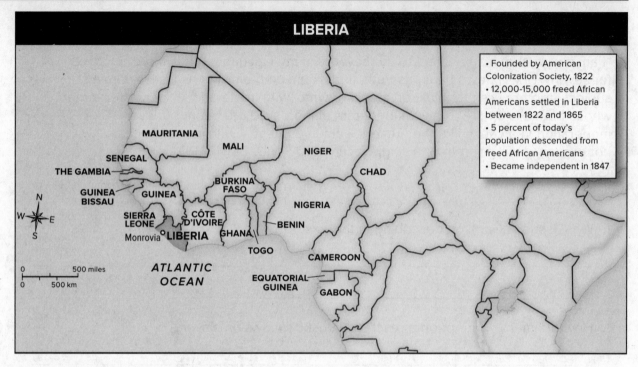

LIBERIA

- Founded by American Colonization Society, 1822
- 12,000-15,000 freed African Americans settled in Liberia between 1822 and 1865
- 5 percent of today's population descended from freed African Americans
- Became independent in 1847

4. Based on the map, which group worked for the establishment of Liberia, a colony for freed African Americans?

_____

5. Based on the map, what is the capital of Liberia?

_____

6. Based on the map, how many freed African Americans settled in Liberia in 1822–1865?

_____

DIRECTIONS: Essay Answer the following question on a separate piece of paper.

7. Describe the opposing views of slavery among Northerners.

Lesson Quiz 16-1

netw🌐rks

Toward Civil War

DIRECTIONS: Matching Match each item with the correct statement below.

_____ 1. name used in 1856 newspaper stories about events in Lawrence, Kansas

_____ 2. put the issue of slavery to popular vote

_____ 3. included the Fugitive Slave Act

_____ 4. the line that marked the division between slave states and non-slave states

_____ 5. violent abolitionist

A. 36° 30' North Latitude

B. "Bleeding Kansas"

C. John Brown

D. Compromise of 1850

E. Kansas-Nebraska Act

DIRECTIONS: Multiple Choice Indicate the answer choice that best completes the statement or answers the question.

_____ 6. The Wilmot Proviso called for

    A. the election of Martin Van Buren.

    B. banning slavery in any lands the U.S. acquired from Mexico.

    C. California entering the Union as a slave state.

    D. a pro-slavery government in Kansas.

_____ 7. What approach did Senator Stephen A. Douglas propose as an alternative to the Missouri Compromise?

    A. Gadsden Purchase

    B. Texas-Maine Act

    C. popular sovereignty

    D. free soil

_____ 8. Which term refers to pro-slavery activists who crossed the Kansas border to vote?

    A. border patrollers   **C.** Iowans

    B. border ruffians   **D.** Missourians

_____ 9. In which state did rival pro-slavery and antislavery governments exist at the same time?

    A. California   **C.** Missouri

    B. Kansas   **D.** Texas

_____ 10. What is the name for a war between citizens of the same country?

    A. civil war   **C.** inter-country war

    B. cold war   **D.** undeclared war

Lesson Quiz 16-2

networks

Toward Civil War

DIRECTIONS: True/False Indicate whether the statement is true or false.

_____ **1.** The Know-Nothings chose Millard Fillmore as their candidate in the 1856 presidential election.

_____ **2.** The American Party grew quickly due to its anti-immigrant views.

_____ **3.** Lincoln believed slavery was moral.

_____ **4.** An arsenal is a storage site for weapons.

_____ **5.** Pro-slavery groups considered John Brown a martyr.

DIRECTIONS: Multiple Choice Indicate the answer choice that best completes the statement or answers the question.

_____ **6.** Which party did the Antislavery Whigs, Democrats, and Free-Soilers join together to form?

    A. Abolitionist Party   **C.** Northern Party

    B. Antislavery Party   **D.** Republican Party

_____ **7.** Which of the following relates to a Supreme Court decision that ruled that the Constitution protected slavery?

    A. Dred Scott   **C.** Lincoln-Douglas

    B. Harpers Ferry   **D.** Missouri Compromise

_____ **8.** Which of these accusations did Douglas make against Lincoln?

    A. Lincoln secretly supported the Freeport Doctrine.

    B. Lincoln wanted African Americans to be fully equal to whites.

    C. Lincoln wanted the United States to abolish popular sovereignty.

    D. Lincoln wanted the United States to return to British rule.

_____ **9.** Who led a raid on a federal arsenal at Harpers Ferry, Virginia?

    A. Abraham Lincoln   **C.** John Brown

    B. Dred Scott   **D.** Stephen A. Douglas

_____ **10.** Lincoln was largely unknown before which election?

    A. 1856 presidential election

    B. 1858 congressional election

    C. 1860 congressional election

    D. 1860 presidential election

Lesson Quiz 16-3

networks

Toward Civil War

DIRECTIONS: Completion Enter the appropriate word(s) to complete the statement.

1. The issue of _____ created a break in the Democratic Party during the 1860 presidential election.

2. Lincoln and _____ other candidates ran for president in 1860.

3. Even though his name was not on the ballot in most Southern states, Lincoln was elected U.S. president because the North was more _____.

4. White Southerners feared that the 1860 victories by Lincoln's _____ Party would result in slave revolts.

5. After the election of Abraham Lincoln to the presidency, the Southern states debated the question of _____, or withdrawing from the Union.

DIRECTIONS: Multiple Choice Indicate the answer choice that best completes the statement or answers the question.

_____ 6. Which was the first state to vote to secede from the Union?

    A. Georgia   **C.** Missouri

    B. Maryland   **D.** South Carolina

_____ 7. Who was the first president of the Confederate States of America?

    A. Abraham Lincoln   **C.** Robert E. Lee

    B. Jefferson Davis   **D.** Stephen Douglas

_____ 8. Which of these concepts did secessionists use to support their views?

    A. constitutionalism   **C.** popular sovereignty

    B. federalism   **D.** states' rights

_____ 9. Which of these was the third state to secede from the Union?

    A. Connecticut

    B. Florida

    C. New York

    D. Ohio

_____ 10. Which event marked the beginning of the Civil War?

    A. attack on Fort Sumter

    B. Lincoln-Douglas debates

    C. Lincoln inauguration

    D. secession of South Carolina

Discovering Our Past: A History of the United States

Chapter 16 Test, Traditional

netw⊙rks

Toward Civil War

DIRECTIONS: True/False Indicate whether the statement is true or false.

_____ **1.** The Whig Party selected Millard Fillmore as a presidential candidate in 1849.

_____ **2.** The Missouri Compromise preserved the balance between slave states and free states.

_____ **3.** The Wilmot Proviso allowed California to enter the Union as a free state.

_____ **4.** John C. Calhoun offered a counter proposal to the Wilmot Proviso.

_____ **5.** Both Zachary Taylor and Lewis Cass ignored the issue of slavery during the 1848 presidential election.

DIRECTIONS: Matching Match each item with the correct statement below.

_____ **6.** won the 1848 presidential election

_____ **7.** arose from the Lincoln-Douglas debates

_____ **8.** wrote "Civil Disobedience"

_____ **9.** wrote the *Dred Scott* decision

_____ **10.** Stephen Douglas's resolution of Henry Clay's slavery plan

A. Compromise of 1850

B. Freeport Doctrine

C. Henry David Thoreau

D. Roger B. Taney

E. Zachary Taylor

DIRECTIONS: Multiple Choice Indicate the answer choice that best completes the statement or answers the question.

_____ **11.** Which of these was the result of enforcement of the Fugitive Slave Act?

    A. anger in the North

    B. compromise on the slavery question

    C. recognition of states' rights

    D. resolution of the slavery question

_____ **12.** Which position did Franklin Pierce begin holding in 1853?

    A. editor of *The Liberator*

    B. chief justice

    C. president of the United States

    D. United States senator

_____ **13.** James Polk and the Democrats favored the annexation of which state?

    A. Maine

    B. Missouri

    C. North Carolina

    D. Texas

_____ **14.** What does *abstain* mean?

    A. to create a network

    B. to leave the Union

    C. to not vote

    D. to vote

_____ **15.** Who was a violent opponent of slavery?

    A. Preston Brooks

    B. John Brown

    C. Andrew P. Butler

    D. Charles Sumner

_____ **16.** What was the main topic of the Lincoln-Douglas debates?

    A. admission of Illinois to the Union

    B. economic issues

    C. slavery

    D. war with Mexico

_____ **17.** Who believed that neither Congress nor local governments had the authority to ban slavery from a territory?

    A. John C. Calhoun

    B. Henry Clay

    C. Zachary Taylor

    D. Daniel Webster

Chapter 16 Test, Traditional *cont.*

netw⊙rks

Toward Civil War

> "Upon these considerations, it is the opinion of the court that the Act of Congress [the Missouri Compromise] which prohibited a citizen from holding and owning property of this kind in the territory of the United States north of the line therein mentioned, is not warranted by the Constitution, and is therefore void; and that neither Dred Scott himself, nor any of his family, were made free by being carried into this territory; even if they had been carried there by the owner, with the intention of becoming a permanent resident."
>
> —Chief Justice Roger B. Taney, *Dred Scott* decision, March 6, 1857

_____ **18.** Which "property of this kind" is being referred to in Taney's decision?

    A. an Act of Congress

    B. Dred Scott and his family

    C. the Missouri Compromise

    D. United States territories

_____ **19.** The South was mostly pleased by the *Dred Scott* decision because the Supreme Court ruled that

    A. Dred Scott could own slaves.

    B. Dred Scott must be freed.

    C. restricting slavery was unconstitutional.

    D. human beings were not property.

_____ **20.** The Supreme Court's ruling in *Scott* v. *Sandford*

    A. was a popular decision throughout the nation.

    B. received almost no support in the South.

    C. outraged opponents of slavery.

    D. was overturned by presidential veto.

DIRECTIONS: Short Answer Answer each of the following questions.

21. How did many Northerners react to the passage of the Fugitive Slave Act?

_____

_____

_____

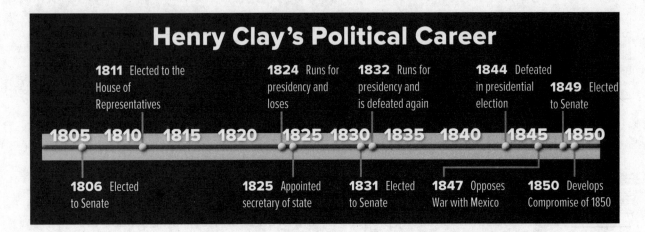
22. How did Henry David Thoreau believe people should deal with unjust laws?

_____

_____

_____

Henry Clay's Political Career

1811 Elected to the House of Representatives

1824 Runs for presidency and loses

1832 Runs for presidency and is defeated again

1844 Defeated in presidential election

1849 Elected to Senate

1805 1810 1815 1820 1825 1830 1835 1840 1845 1850

1806 Elected to Senate

1825 Appointed secretary of state

1831 Elected to Senate

1847 Opposes War with Mexico

1850 Develops Compromise of 1850

23. According to the time line, how many Senate terms did Henry Clay serve?

_____

_____

24. According to the time line, in which presidential elections did Clay run?

_____

_____

DIRECTIONS: Essay Answer the following question.

25. *Sectionalism* is a term for an exaggerated loyalty to a particular part of the country. How did sectionalism lead to the Civil War?

_____

_____

_____

_____

Chapter 16 Test, Document-Based Questions

netw⊙rks

Toward Civil War

DIRECTIONS: Short Answer Answer each of the following questions on a separate piece of paper.

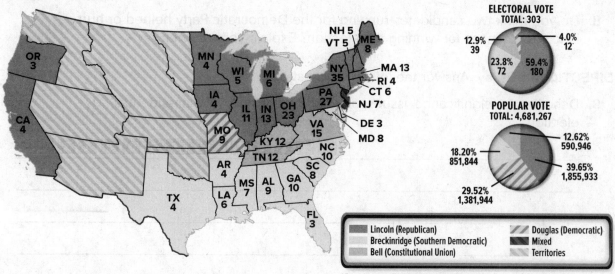

ELECTORAL VOTE
TOTAL: 303

12.9% 39
4.0% 12
23.8% 72
59.4% 180

POPULAR VOTE
TOTAL: 4,681,267

12.62% 590,946
18.20% 851,844
39.65% 1,855,933
29.52% 1,381,944

	Lincoln (Republican)		Douglas (Democratic)
	Breckinridge (Southern Democratic)		Mixed
	Bell (Constitutional Union)		Territories

* Four electors in New Jersey voted for Lincoln and three voted for Douglas.

1. According to the circle graphs, who received the fewest electoral votes in the 1860 presidential election?

2. Who received the largest portion of the popular vote?

3. Which candidate had the greatest percentage increase from electoral votes to popular votes?

4. Which candidate received the smallest portion of the popular vote?

5. According to the map, in which region did Breckinridge win?

6. Which state had the most electoral votes?

7. Lincoln was elected president even though he received less than half of the popular vote. Explain why Lincoln won the election.

8. Do you think two candidates running for the Democratic Party helped or hurt Lincoln's chances for winning the election? Explain your answer.

DIRECTIONS: Essay Answer the following question.

9. Describe the significance, issues, and outcome of the 1860 presidential election.

_____

_____

_____

_____

_____

_____

_____

_____

_____

_____

_____

_____

_____

_____

_____

_____

_____

Lesson Quiz 17-1

netw⊚rks

The Civil War

DIRECTIONS: True/False Indicate whether the statement is true or false.

_____ **1.** Maryland, Delaware, Kentucky, and Missouri had close ties to both the Union and the Confederacy.

_____ **2.** Slavery was banned in the border states.

_____ **3.** An efficient railway network was one of the South's strengths.

_____ **4.** For the South, the primary aim of the war was to preserve slavery.

_____ **5.** For the North, the primary goal was to preserve the Union.

DIRECTIONS: Multiple Choice Indicate the answer choice that best completes the statement or answers the question.

_____ **6.** Which was the most vital border state for the Union?

    A. Delaware

    B. Kentucky

    C. Maryland

    D. Missouri

_____ **7.** The South expected support from Britain and France because these two European nations relied on the South for

    A. cotton.

    B. rice.

    C. manufactured goods.

    D. goods and services.

_____ **8.** What was one of the main advantages of the South?

    A. a larger population

    B. excellent military leaders

    C. belief in states' rights

    D. strong industries

_____ **9.** From where did most Confederate and Union soldiers come?

    A. cities

    B. farms

    C. the far West

    D. coastal areas

Lesson Quiz 17-2

networks

The Civil War

DIRECTIONS: Completion Enter the appropriate word(s) to complete the statement.

1. General _____ headed the Union army of the East after the Battle of Bull Run.

2. The Confederacy used ironclads to _____ their harbors and rivers.

3. The _____ and the *Monitor* took part in a battle that raised spirits in the North and in the South.

4. A key victory for the North was when Union naval forces under David Farragut captured _____ on April 25, 1862.

DIRECTIONS: Multiple Choice Indicate the answer choice that best answers the question.

_____ 5. Where was the first major battle of the Civil War?

    A. Antietam Creek

    B. Bull Run

    C. Richmond

    D. Shiloh

_____ 6. Who was the Union general who captured Fort Henry?

    A. David Farragut

    B. George B. McClellan

    C. Robert E. Lee

    D. Ulysses S. Grant

_____ 7. What was the Union goal in the West?

    A. to control California

    B. to control Texas

    C. to control the Mississippi River

    D. to control the Tennessee River

_____ 8. Together the Union and Confederate armies suffered more than 23,000 casualties in which battle?

    A. Bull Run

    B. New Orleans

    C. Richmond

    D. Shiloh

Discovering Our Past: A History of the United States

Lesson Quiz 17-3

networks

The Civil War

DIRECTIONS: Matching Match each item with the correct statement below.

_____ **1.** legal order that guarantees a prisoner the right to be heard in court

_____ **2.** Southern spy

_____ **3.** Northerner who helped wounded soldiers

_____ **4.** called "Copperheads" by critics

_____ **5.** payments to encourage enlistment

A. Clara Barton

B. Peace Democrats

C. Rose O'Neal Greenhow

D. bounties

E. habeas corpus

DIRECTIONS: Multiple Choice Indicate the answer choice that best answers the question.

_____ **6.** Why did the South suffer most of the destruction during the Civil War?

  A. because most battles were fought in Georgia

  B. because most of the fighting took place there

  C. because schools and churches were used as hospitals

  D. because of its extensive railroad mileage

_____ **7.** Which type of law required Confederate men between certain ages to serve in the army for three years?

  A. bounty

  B. corpus

  C. draft

  D. habeas corpus

_____ **8.** Which Northern city saw the most violent opposition to laws requiring military service?

  A. Charleston

  B. New York City

  C. Richmond

  D. Washington, D.C.

_____ **9.** To raise money for the war, what did the North print?

  A. greenbacks

  B. handbills

  C. paper checks

  D. promissory notes

Lesson Quiz 17-4

networks

The Civil War

DIRECTIONS: True/False Indicate whether the statement is true or false.

_____ **1.** Stonewall Jackson was killed at the Battle of Gettysburg.

_____ **2.** Lincoln replaced General George McClellan with General Ambrose Burnside.

_____ **3.** The Union army was composed mostly of African American soldiers.

_____ **4.** The Gettysburg Address was given at a ceremony to dedicate a cemetery.

_____ **5.** The 54th Massachusetts was an all-female regiment.

DIRECTIONS: Multiple Choice Indicate the answer choice that best completes the statement or answers the question.

_____ **6.** Confederate leaders hoped that a victory in Union territory would win support from

    A. Britain and France.

    B. France and Spain.

    C. Spain and Britain.

    D. Spain and Germany.

_____ **7.** General Grant led a 47-day siege against which city?

    A. Atlanta, Georgia

    B. Mobile, Alabama

    C. Port Hudson, Louisiana

    D. Vicksburg, Mississippi

_____ **8.** By the end of the war, African American volunteers made up nearly which percentage of the Union army?

    A. 10 percent

    B. 20 percent

    C. 50 percent

    D. 100 percent

_____ **9.** President Lincoln's address at which battlefield honored soldiers and stated his vision for the country?

    A. Chancellorsville

    B. Gettysburg

    C. Shiloh

    D. Vicksburg

Discovering Our Past: A History of the United States

Lesson Quiz 17-5

networks

The Civil War

DIRECTIONS: Completion Enter the appropriate word(s) to complete the statement.

1. Because of the huge loss of life among his own troops, critics of
_____ in the North called him a "butcher."

2. In November 1864, Abraham Lincoln defeated _____
and won reelection.

3. The formal end of the war came on April 9, _____.

4. The Civil War made it clear that the national government was more powerful than the
government of _____.

DIRECTIONS: Multiple Choice Indicate the answer choice that best answers the question.

_____ 5. Which of the following is the systematic destruction of an entire land—not just
an army?

   A. blockade

   B. slash-and-burn

   C. terminal war

   D. total war

_____ 6. What helped Lincoln win the 1864 election?

   A. Lee's surrender

   B. promotion of Grant

   C. Sherman's capture of Atlanta

   D. winning at Gettysburg

_____ 7. What was Sherman's march across Georgia toward the Atlantic called?

   A. Cold War

   B. Long Siege

   C. March to the Atlantic

   D. March to the Sea

_____ 8. Where did General Robert E. Lee surrender to General Ulysses S. Grant?

   A. Appomattox Court House

   B. Gettysburg Cemetery

   C. Richmond

   D. Vicksburg

Chapter 17 Test, Traditional

netw⬤rks

The Civil War

DIRECTIONS: True/False Indicate whether the statement is true or false.

_____ **1.** The basic strategy of the Confederacy was to conduct a defensive war.

_____ **2.** The Union won a narrow victory at the Battle of Shiloh.

_____ **3.** When the Civil War began, many teenagers stayed home and did not serve in the military.

_____ **4.** Sherman's March to the Sea ended in a defeat for the Union.

_____ **5.** The 54th Massachusetts regiment served with distinction at Fort Wagner and in the Battle of Olustee.

DIRECTIONS: Matching Match each item with the correct statement below.

_____ **6.** Union soldiers   **A.** casualties

_____ **7.** refusal to give in   **B.** Yankees

_____ **8.** people killed or wounded   **C.** Rebels

_____ **9.** Confederate soldiers   **D.** entrenched

_____ **10.** in a protected position   **E.** resistance

DIRECTIONS: Multiple Choice Indicate the answer choice that best completes the statement or answers the question.

> "No terms except unconditional and immediate surrender can be accepted."
>
> —at the capture of Fort Donelson, February 16, 1862

_____ **11.** This quotation provided a nickname for which Northern hero?

 A. Albert Sidney Johnson

 B. David Farragut

 C. George McClellan

 D. Ulysses S. Grant

> "[They] will make good soldiers and taking them from the enemy weakens him in the same proportion they strengthen us."
>
> —Ulysses S. Grant, letter to Abraham Lincoln, August 23, 1863

_____ **12.** In this excerpt from a letter written by General Grant to President Lincoln, to whom is Grant referring?

 A. African Americans

 B. female spies

 C. Native Americans

 D. teenagers

_____ **13.** Because the war disrupted their supply of cotton, the South expected support from which two countries?

 A. Britain and France

 B. France and Canada

 C. France and Spain

 D. Spain and Mexico

Chapter 17 Test, Traditional *cont.*

The Civil War

_____ **14.** Who convinced officials to let women work as nurses and recruited many women to serve as nurses during the Civil War?

   A. Dorothea Dix

   B. Frances Clayton

   C. President Lincoln

   D. Rose O'Neal Greenhow

_____ **15.** Who or what was the *Merrimack*?

   A. a battle near Bull Run in Northern Virginia

   B. a damaged ship that was rebuilt and covered with iron by the Confederates

   C. a victory for the Confederate forces in the East

   D. a soldier who was killed in battle

_____ **16.** Why did the Union want to control the Mississippi River and its tributaries?

   A. The Union army lacked battle experience.

   B. to increase enlistment

   C. to capture Confederate ships

   D. to prevent supplies from reaching the eastern Confederacy

_____ **17.** Which of these cities was the capital of the Confederacy?

   A. Baltimore, Maryland

   B. Washington, D.C.

   C. Spotsylvania, Virginia

   D. Richmond, Virginia

_____ **18.** The leadership of which two generals was a key factor in the Confederates' military success in the East?

   A. Ambrose Burnside and Joseph Hooker

   B. George McClellan and George Meade

   C. Ambrose Burnside and Ulysses S. Grant

   D. Robert E. Lee and Stonewall Jackson

_____ **19.** Among the abolitionists who urged Lincoln to make the Civil War a fight to end slavery were Frederick Douglass and

   A. James Buchanan.   **C.** Horace Greeley.

   B. William T. Sherman.   **D.** Winfield Scott.

Chapter 17 Test, Traditional *cont.*

The Civil War

DIRECTIONS: Short Answer Answer each of the following questions.

> "In the time I am writing, every stalk of corn in [cornfields to the north] was cut as closely as could have been done with a knife, and the slain lay in rows precisely as they had stood in their ranks a few minutes before."
>
> —a Union officer

20. Which battle, that resulted in the single deadliest day of the Civil War, is being described in this excerpt?

_____

> "It had suddenly appeared to him that perhaps in a battle he might run. He was forced to admit that as far as war was concerned he knew nothing of himself. . . . A little panic-fear grew in his mind. As his imagination went forward to a fight, he saw hideous possibilities."
>
> —Stephen Crane, *The Red Badge of Courage*

21. In this excerpt from *The Red Badge of Courage*, what tells you that the character is afraid?

_____

_____

_____

22. Why was the border state of Maryland vital to the Union?

_____

_____

_____

23. What was the claim to fame of the 54th Massachusetts regiment?

_____

_____

_____

DIRECTIONS: Essay Answer the following question on a separate piece of paper.

24. Why was President Lincoln reluctant at first to emancipate enslaved African Americans? Why did he decide to issue the Emancipation Proclamation?

Chapter 17 Test, Document-Based Questions

networks

The Civil War

DIRECTIONS: Short Answer Answer each of the following questions on a separate piece of paper.

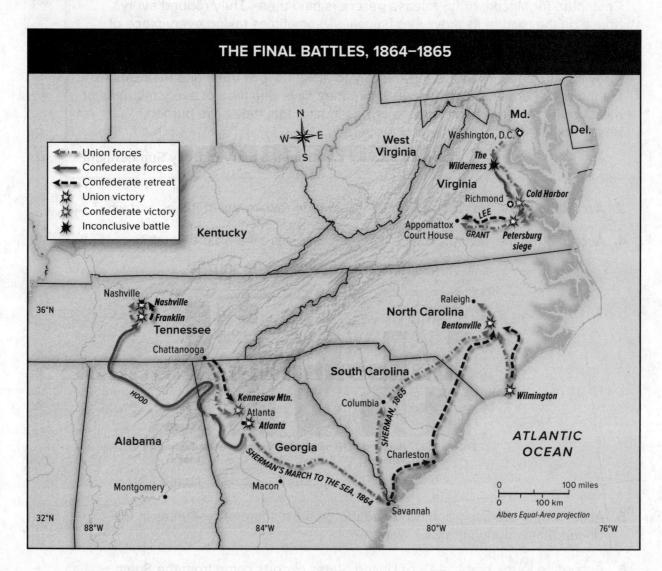

THE FINAL BATTLES, 1864–1865

1. According to the map, which state saw a Union victory, a Confederate victory, and an indecisive battle?

2. Based on the Final Battles map, what was the result of the siege of Petersburg?

The Civil War

"July 29, 1864—Sleepless nights. The report is that the Yankees have left Covington for Macon, . . . to release prisoners held there. They robbed every house on the road of its provisions [supplies], sometimes taking every piece of meat, blankets and wearing apparel, silver and arms of every description. They would take silk dresses and put them under their saddles, and many other things for which they had no use. Is this the way to make us love them and their Union? Let the poor people answer [those] whom they have deprived of every mouthful of meat and of their livestock to make any! Our mills, too, they have burned, destroying an immense amount of property."

—from the diary of Dolly Sumner Lunt

3. According to the excerpt, what is Lunt's attitude toward the Yankees and why?

4. According to the excerpt, what toll did the Civil War take on the South?

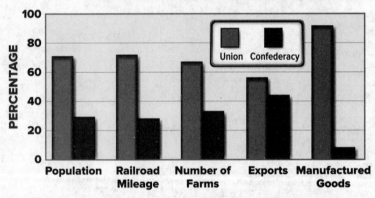

RESOURCES IN THE NORTH AND SOUTH

Source: U.S. Census Bureau, *Historical Statistics of the United States*

5. According to the bar graph, who had the greatest share of resources in the United States during the Civil War era?

6. According to the graph, 44% of United States exports came from the South. What important Southern export was disrupted during the Civil War? Which two countries suffered from the disruption?

DIRECTIONS: Essay Answer the following question on a separate piece of paper.

7. Discuss the differences between the North and South that contributed to the course and outcome of the Civil War.

Lesson Quiz 18-1

netw⊙rks

The Reconstruction Era

DIRECTIONS: Matching Match each item with the correct statement below.

_____ **1.** amnesty

_____ **2.** radical

_____ **3.** assassinated President Lincoln

_____ **4.** leading Radical Republican

_____ **5.** outlawed slavery

A. John Wilkes Booth

B. the Thirteenth Amendment

C. extreme

D. a group pardon

E. Thaddeus Stevens

DIRECTIONS: Multiple Choice Indicate the answer choice that best completes the statement or answers the question.

_____ **6.** The period of rebuilding the South after the Civil War was called

   A. amnesty.   **C.** Reconstruction.

   B. Civil Rebuilding.   **D.** war spoils.

_____ **7.** What was the name of the decree that required a majority of the white males in a state to swear loyalty to the Union?

   A. Freedmen's Bureau   **C.** Ten Percent Plan

   B. Reconstruction Act   **D.** Wade-Davis Bill

_____ **8.** Which of these helped African Americans make the transition from slavery to freedom?

   A. Freedmen's Bureau   **C.** Ten Percent Plan

   B. Reconstruction Act   **D.** Wade-Davis Bill

_____ **9.** President Abraham Lincoln was shot at

   A. Ford's Theater.

   B. Samuel Mudd's house.

   C. the White House.

   D. William Peterson's house.

_____ **10.** Who was the only Southern senator to support the Union during the Civil War?

   A. Andrew Jackson

   B. Andrew Johnson

   C. Daniel Webster

   D. John C. Calhoun

Lesson Quiz 18-2

networks

The Reconstruction Era

DIRECTIONS: Completion Enter the appropriate word(s) to complete the statement.

1. _____ were intended to control freed African American men and women.

2. In 1866 President Johnson vetoed both the Freedmen's Bureau bill and the _____.

3. Congress was able to _____ Johnson's vetoes of civil rights legislation.

4. The Fourteenth and Fifteenth Amendments were intended to guarantee newly established rights for _____.

5. The _____ Act prohibited the president from removing government officials without the Senate's approval.

DIRECTIONS: Multiple Choice Indicate the answer choice that best completes the statement or answers the question.

_____ 6. Anyone born in the United States is automatically a citizen, according to the

    A. black codes.

    B. Civil Rights Act of 1866.

    C. Fourteenth Amendment.

    D. Thirteenth Amendment.

_____ 7. In 1867 states that had not ratified the Fourteenth Amendment were required to

    A. elect African American leaders.

    B. form new governments.

    C. leave the United States.

    D. lose their civil rights.

_____ 8. Which Southern state immediately ratified the Fourteenth Amendment?

    A. Kentucky   **C.** North Carolina

    B. Maryland   **D.** Tennessee

_____ 9. When President Andrew Johnson violated the Tenure of Office Act, the House of Representatives voted to

    A. execute him.

    B. impeach him.

    C. reelect him.

    D. suspend him.

Lesson Quiz 18-3

networks

The Reconstruction Era

DIRECTIONS: True/False Indicate whether the statement is true or false.

_____ **1.** Most newly freed African American voters supported the Republican Party.

_____ **2.** Hiram Revels was the first African American to serve as a presidential adviser.

_____ **3.** A scalawag who moved to the North was considered a carpetbagger.

_____ **4.** Many Reconstruction-era Democrats supported the Ku Klux Klan.

_____ **5.** Some freed African Americans borrowed money from the Freedmen's Bank to buy land.

DIRECTIONS: Multiple Choice Indicate the answer choice that best completes the statement or answers the question.

_____ **6.** Southern whites who supported Republican policy throughout Reconstruction were sometimes called

    A. carpetbaggers.   **C.** Republican hostages.

    B. freedmen.   **D.** scalawags.

_____ **7.** Northerners who moved to the South and supported the Republicans were called

    A. carpetbaggers.   **C.** Republican scalawags.

    B. freedmen.   **D.** sharecroppers.

_____ **8.** For a brief time during Reconstruction, African Americans had a majority of seats in the lower house of which state's legislature?

    A. Alabama   **C.** South Carolina

    B. Ohio   **D.** Tennessee

_____ **9.** Which method did some white Southerners use to try to overcome Republican rule?

    A. civil rights legislation   **C.** violence

    B. cooperation   **D.** voting reform

_____ **10.** Which of the following did many African American workers find to be little better than slavery?

    A. integration

    B. land ownership

    C. moving north

    D. sharecropping

Lesson Quiz 18-4

networks

The Reconstruction Era

DIRECTIONS: Matching Match each item with the correct statement below.

_____ 1. rule used to prevent newly freed African Americans from voting

_____ 2. African American civil rights leader

_____ 3. war hero and two-term president

_____ 4. murder by a mob

_____ 5. legally enforced separation of races

A. Ulysses S. Grant

B. lynching

C. W.E.B. Du Bois

D. segregation

E. grandfather clause

DIRECTIONS: Multiple Choice Indicate the answer choice that best completes the statement or answers the question.

_____ 6. Reconstruction effectively ended after the

    A. 1875 Civil Rights Act.

    B. election of Hayes as president.

    C. Republican Party dissolved.

    D. Southern Democrats disbanded.

_____ 7. To keep poor people and African Americans from voting, many Southern states enforced

    A. crop taxes.

    B. Jim Crow laws.

    C. poll taxes.

    D. Reconstruction taxes.

_____ 8. Which type of society did Jim Crow laws enforce?

    A. affluent   **C.** poor

    B. integrated   **D.** segregated

_____ 9. The Ku Klux Klan set out to terrorize

    A. Democratic voters.   **C.** the "New South."

    B. African Americans and   **D.** white voters.
        Republican voters.

_____ 10. Which of these was used to prevent African Americans from voting?

    A. commissions   **C.** literacy tests

    B. integration   **D.** Reconstruction

Chapter 18 Test, Traditional

netw⊙rks

The Reconstruction Era

DIRECTIONS: True/False Indicate whether the statement is true or false.

_____ **1.** The period following the Civil War is known as "the Rebuilding Time."

_____ **2.** Frederick Douglass was born to freed African Americans and was therefore free himself.

_____ **3.** The Ten Percent Plan required ten percent of each state's voters to swear loyalty to the Confederacy.

_____ **4.** President Lincoln was assassinated while attending a play.

_____ **5.** The Wade-Davis Bill replaced the Ten Percent Plan.

DIRECTIONS: Matching Match each item with the correct statement below.

_____ **6.** African American senator

_____ **7.** dishonest or illegal use of authority

_____ **8.** racist secret society

_____ **9.** helped provide education for African Americans

_____ **10.** racially diverse

A. Freedmen's Bureau

B. Ku Klux Klan

C. integrated

D. corruption

E. Blanche K. Bruce

DIRECTIONS: Multiple Choice Indicate the answer choice that best completes the statement or answers the question.

_____ **11.** How did Andrew Johnson become president?

    A. He was selected by the House of Representatives.

    B. He was elected in 1864.

    C. He succeeded Lincoln after Lincoln was assassinated.

    D. Southerners demanded it in the Compromise of 1877.

_____ **12.** What did Congress pass to prevent the president from firing government officials without the Senate's approval?

    A. black codes

    B. Impeachment Act

    C. overrides

    D. Tenure of Office Act

_____ **13.** When Congress did not approve the suspension of Edwin Stanton, what did President Johnson do?

    A. demoted Stanton

    B. fired Stanton

    C. impeached Stanton

    D. resigned the presidency

_____ **14.** When President Johnson violated the Tenure of Office Act, what did Congress do?

    A. demoted Johnson

    B. fired Johnson

    C. impeached Johnson

    D. supported Johnson

_____ **15.** Which of these was a leading industry of the New South?

    A. dairy farming

    B. music

    C. printing

    D. textiles

_____ **16.** Which of these were laws designed to limit the freedom of the newly freed African Americans?

    A. black codes

    B. impeachment

    C. Wade-Davis Bill

    D. Ten Percent Plan

_____ **17.** Which of these was used to violate the civil rights of African Americans?

    A. integration

    B. Exodusters

    C. poll tax

    D. Reconstruction

Chapter 18 Test, Traditional *cont.*

networks

The Reconstruction Era

> "All persons born or naturalized in the United States, and subject to the jurisdiction thereof, are citizens of the United States and of the State wherein they reside. No State shall make or enforce any law which shall abridge the privileges or immunities of citizens of the United States; nor shall any State deprive any person of life, liberty, or property, without due process of law; nor deny to any person within its jurisdiction the equal protection of the laws."

_____ **18.** This definition of U.S. citizenship and description of citizens' rights is from which amendment?

    A. First Amendment

    B. Fifth Amendment

    C. Twelfth Amendment

    D. Fourteenth Amendment

_____ **19.** Which earlier legislation was this amendment intended to protect?

    A. black codes

    B. the 1866 Civil Rights Act

    C. the Fugitive Slave Act

    D. the Radical Republican Act

_____ **20.** What does the amendment say state governments cannot take from citizens without due process?

    A. life, liberty, and property

    B. the right to bear arms

    C. immunity to federal laws

    D. freedom of speech

Chapter 18 Test, Traditional *cont.*

netw⊙rks

The Reconstruction Era

DIRECTIONS: Short Answer Answer each of the following questions.

African Americans in the United States Congress, late 1800s					
Year	No. of Members	States Represented	Year	No. of Members	States Represented
1870	2	SC, GA	1883	1	NC
1871	4	SC, AL, FL	1889	1	NC
1873	4	AL, SC, MI	1890	2	VA, SC
1875	4	AL, NC, LA, SC	1893	1	SC
1877	1	SC	1896	1	SC
1882	1	NC	1897	1	NC

21. According to the chart, which states had the first African American members of Congress?

_____

22. According to the chart, in which year did Florida elect its first African American member of Congress?

_____

23. According to the chart, which period saw the highest African American membership in Congress?

_____

24. According to the chart, which state was most often represented by African Americans?

_____

25. What were the requirements for a state to rejoin the Union under the Wade-Davis Bill?

_____

_____

_____

Chapter 18 Test, Document-Based Questions   **netw⊙rks**

DIRECTIONS: Multiple Choice Indicate the answer choice that best completes the statement or answers the question.

"The military rule which [the First Reconstruction Act] establishes is plainly to be used, not for any purpose of order or for the prevention of crime, but solely as a means of coercing the people into the adoption of principles and measures to which it is known that they are opposed, and upon which they have an undeniable right to exercise their own judgment.

"I submit to Congress whether this measure is not in . . . palpable conflict with the plainest provisions of the Constitution, and utterly destructive to those great principles of liberty and humanity for which our ancestors on both sides of the Atlantic have shed so much blood and expended so much treasure."

—President Andrew Johnson, 1867

_____ **1.** This excerpt, from a message to Congress by Johnson, argues that the First Reconstruction Act

    A. is necessary to maintain order in the South.

    B. is unconstitutional.

    C. will help African Americans achieve equality.

    D. will speed economic recovery in the North.

Chapter 18 Test, Document-Based Questions *cont.*

networks

The Reconstruction Era

DIRECTIONS: Short Answer Answer each of the following questions on a separate piece of paper.

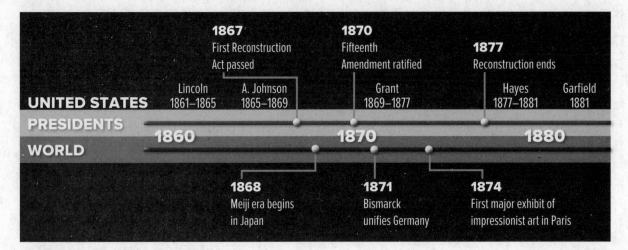

2. According to the time line and your readings, how many U.S. presidents presided over Reconstruction?

3. For about what length of time was federal Reconstruction legislation passed after the Lincoln Administration?

4. Between which two U.S. events would ratification of the Fourteenth Amendment be placed?

5. During whose presidential administration was the Fifteenth Amendment ratified?

6. Which national event coincided with the end of Reconstruction?

7. Which presidents on the time line served after the end of Reconstruction?

8. What were the results of the 1874 Congressional elections and how did they weaken support for African American rights?

Discovering Our Past: A History of the United States

CHAPTER 1

LESSON QUIZ 1-1
Matching

  1. d   **2.** b   **3.** e   **4.** a   **5.** c

Multiple Choice

  6. b   **7.** c   **8.** b   **9.** c   **10.** a

LESSON QUIZ 1-2
True/False

  1. True

  2. False

  3. True

  4. False

  5. False

Multiple Choice

  6. a   **7.** d   **8.** c   **9.** b   **10.** b

LESSON QUIZ 1-3
Completion

  1. The Four Corners

  2. northernmost (or northern)

  3. adobe

  4. Grand Council

Multiple Choice

  5. b   **6.** c   **7.** a   **8.** a

CHAPTER 1 TEST, TRADITIONAL
True/False

  1. False

  2. True

  3. True

  4. False

  5. False

Matching

  6. a   **7.** d   **8.** b   **9.** c   **10.** e

Multiple Choice

  11. b   **12.** a   **13.** b   **14.** c   **15.** a

  16. b   **17.** c   **18.** c   **19.** b   **20.** d

Short Answer

  21. Mexico

  22. the Olmec; for about 1,200 years

  23. the Aztec; for about 221 years

  24. the Inca; between 450 and 500 years ago

Essay

  25. Correct answers should include three of the following: Native peoples depended on their environments for food, shelter, and clothing. The Hohokam modified their environment by digging irrigation channels to water their fields. The Anasazi modified the stone and atural cliffs to build safe homes and cities. The Inuit wore seal skins to protect themselves from the climate. The Plains peoples were nomads, following the food sources. The peoples of the Northwest ate salmon they caught in the nearby rivers.

CHAPTER 1 TEST, DOCUMENT-BASED QUESTIONS
Short Answer

  1. His dog is howling and his chickens are dancing.

  2. The "stomp dance" must have been something unique to the Natchez people.

  3. The dog in the story talks.

  4. Possible answer: "Prehistoric Migration in the Americas"

  5. Possible answers include: Beringia, the Bering Strait, present-day Alaska

  6. southward

Essay

  7. Correct answers should include: Early peoples probably came from Asia across a land bridge called Beringia, which appeared during the Ice Age due to low sea levels. (They also may have crossed the ice or taken boats during periods when the land bridge was submerged under water.) The bridge/route linked Siberia to North America. They most likely came in search of food, possibly following the hunt for mammoths or other large game. As their numbers grew, they migrated southward. Their cultures changed as they migrated due to the different types of environments they encountered (climate, local wildlife, terrain, and so on).

CHAPTER 2

LESSON QUIZ 2-1

Completion

1. caravel
2. Crusades
3. Islam
4. "rebirth"

Multiple Choice

5. a   6. a   7. b   8. b

LESSON QUIZ 2-2

True/False

1. False
2. False
3. True
4. True

Multiple Choice

5. c   6. d   7. c   8. d

LESSON QUIZ 2-3

Matching

1. b   2. d   3. a   4. c   5. e

Multiple Choice

6. a   7. b   8. c   9. a

LESSON QUIZ 2-4

True/False

1. True
2. True
3. False

Multiple Choice

4. c   5. a   6. b   7. c   8. a

CHAPTER 2 TEST, TRADITIONAL

True/False

1. True
2. True
3. True
4. False
5. True

Matching

6. a   7. c   8. a   9. b   10. b

Multiple Choice

11. c   12. c   13. a   14. a   15. b
16. b   17. b   18. a   19. c

Short Answer

20. presidios, pueblos, missions

21. tenant farmer

22. one: signed Treaty of Tordesillas

23. Correct answers should include: Spain was interested in wealth, settlements, and spreading Christianity. Portugal wished to increase trade.

CHAPTER 2 TEST, DOCUMENT-BASED QUESTIONS

Short Answer

1. Columbus is referring to Queen Isabella of Spain.

2. Correct answers should include: Columbus is referring to a flag. He has planted the Spanish flag on the lands he has claimed for the queen.

3. Magellan's crew finished their voyage between the time when Luther promoted reform of the Catholic Church and Cartier claimed Canada for France.

4. Thirteen years passed between the settlement of Jamestown and the founding of the Plymouth.

5. Cartier and Verrazano sailed for France.

6. Of the explorers shown, Christopher Columbus sailed farthest west.

Essay

7. Correct answers should include: Exploration was important for many reasons. Finding new routes at sea led to the discovery of new lands, as well as shorter, safer paths to the nations already known. Exploration often led to trade with other nations, including the trade of goods, services, knowledge, and scientific inventions. Exploration also led to new sources of natural resources for the nation that claimed the new land.

CHAPTER 3

LESSON QUIZ 3-1

Completion

1. Croatoan Island
2. profits
3. burgesses
4. women
5. royal

Multiple Choice

6. c   **7.** d   **8.** c   **9.** c   **10.** a

LESSON QUIZ 3-2
True/False

1. False
2. False
3. True
4. True
5. True

Multiple Choice

6. c   **7.** a   **8.** d   **9.** a   **10.** d

LESSON QUIZ 3-3
Matching

1. d   **2.** a   **3.** c   **4.** b   **5.** e

Multiple Choice

6. b   **7.** c   **8.** c   **9.** c   **10.** a

LESSON QUIZ 3-4
Completion

1. Indentured
2. Virginia
3. Africa
4. Native Americans
5. Georgia

Multiple Choice

6. b   **7.** b   **8.** a   **9.** a

CHAPTER 3 TEST, TRADITIONAL
True/False

1. False
2. True
3. True
4. False
5. True

Matching

6. b   **7.** c   **8.** a   **9.** d   **10.** e

Multiple Choice

11. c   **12.** b   **13.** d   **14.** c   **15.** a
16. a   **17.** b   **18.** b

Short Answer

19. Maryland and Georgia

20. 6

21. "playful one"

22. democratic or representative

Essay

23. Correct answers should include: The Quakers did not believe in war or violence. This would have put them at odds with countrymen who believed that the British Empire should be preserved and expanded, through violence if necessary. The Quakers also believed that each person has an "inner light" to guide them. This would have put them at odds with those who believed that people should follow rules set down by churches or governments. The British also had a strong class consciousness, and many of them probably took exception to the Quaker beliefs that people are all equal and deserving of equal rights and opportunities (that a King was as worthy as a commoner).

CHAPTER 3 TEST, DOCUMENT-BASED QUESTIONS
Short Answer

1. Correct answers should include: The overseer tied people up and flogged them, then poured brine on their wounds and made them stay that way all day.

2. Correct answers should include: to make certain enslaved people worked (and did not run away).

3. Possible answers: Grandy seems to be detached and emotionless; he is writing the facts and does not give his opinion; one might expect him to express very strong emotions like disgust or hate.

4. 1690–1710

5. 1690–1710

6. the South

Essay

7. Correct answers should include an overview of the origins and growth of slavery in the Colonies. Mention should be made of the institution's economic underpinnings (especially in the Southern Colonies) and its racial component.

CHAPTER 4
LESSON QUIZ 4-1
Matching

1. d	**2.** c	**3.** a	**4.** e	**5.** b

Multiple Choice

6. c	**7.** c	**8.** d	**9.** b	**10.** c

LESSON QUIZ 4-2
True/False

1. False

2. True

3. False

4. True

5. False

Matching

6. e	**7.** c	**8.** a	**9.** b	**10.** d

LESSON QUIZ 4-3
Multiple Choice

1. c	**2.** c	**3.** b	**4.** c	**5.** b

Short Answer

6. religion, education, and science

7. Zenger's libel case against the *New York Journal*

8. They learned at home, taught by their parents.

9. They ran households, cared for children, and worked in the fields with their husbands.

10. Civic virtue refers to democratic ideas, practices, and values.

LESSON QUIZ 4-4
Matching

1. d	**2.** a	**3.** a	**4.** c	**5.** d

Short Answer

6. Six nations: the Mohawk, Seneca, Cayuga, Onondaga, Oneida, and Tuscarora.

7. The colonies did not support the plan.

8. They had a strong connection through the fur trade. The French did not want to take over Native American land. Many French trappers and traders married Native American women. Finally, many Native Americans converted to Catholicism through French missionaries.

9. Great Britain would pay for it and then increase the taxes of the colonists to help pay off the debt.

10. They lost their French allies. The British forced them to pay higher prices for goods and did not pay Native Americans to use their land. Many English colonists began settling on Native American land.

CHAPTER 4 TEST, TRADITIONAL
True/False

1. True

2. False

3. True

4. True

5. False

Matching

6. d	**7.** a	**8.** c	**9.** b	**10.** e

Multiple Choice

11. d	**12.** c	**13.** d	**14.** c	**15.** a
16. a	**17.** d	**18.** d	**19.** b	

Short Answer

20. Correct answers should include: Virginia seems a promising but not yet completely developed place, in Andrew Burnaby's view. It possesses great resources, plenty of good land and produces large quantities of grain, cattle, and a variety of fruit. It is as yet not fully exploited in terms of agricultural possibilities, but already its pork is superb and its impressive horses are fast and beautiful.

21. New York and Philadelphia

22. Answers may vary but should include: enslaved people were not allowed to leave the plantation; it was illegal to allow them to learn how to read and write; they were not allowed to assemble; punishments were whipping, hanging, and burning for various things, including running away.

23. West Indies

Essay

24. Correct answers should include: The side that received the best trade terms from Native Americans and the most help in war would probably win the contest for the control of North America. The French had the advantage. Unlike the British, the French were more interested in trading furs than taking over the Native Americans' land. The French had better relations with Native Americans. Many French trappers and fur traders married Native American women and followed their customs. French missionaries converted many Native Americans to Catholicism but let them maintain their own culture.

CHAPTER 4 TEST, DOCUMENT-BASED QUESTIONS
Short Answer

1. Correct answers should include: They were taken without their consent from their parents and their native land.

2. Correct answers should include: their home in a plentiful country, their friends and family in Africa, and their ability to create lasting family ties in the colonies.

3. Correct answers should include: They believe they share a natural right to freedom.

4. Correct answers should include: Colonists entered the slave trade for economic reasons: they needed a large labor force to grow cash crops such as tobacco and rice.

5. Correct answers should include: They had to set aside their belief in the rights and liberty for all people, because slavery denied those rights to Africans.

Essay

6. Correct answers should include: The colonists and the enslaved people had very different experiences. The colonists chose to come to North America from Europe. They enjoyed basic human rights, including the right to vote (for landowning men) and govern themselves to a certain extent. Enslaved people were Africans who were kidnapped and brought to North America and forced to work for whites. They had few basic rights, not even the right to get

married or raise their own children. Although the colonists had far more freedom than the enslaved people, their rights to govern themselves and certain economic rights were limited by English rule.

CHAPTER 5
LESSON QUIZ 5-1
Completion
1. French and Indian War
2. court
3. Stamp Act
4. effigies
5. Correct answers should include: boycotting British products, wearing home-made clothing, forming the Daughters of Liberty.

Multiple Choice
6. c **7.** c **8.** b **9.** d **10.** a

LESSON QUIZ 5-2
True/False
1. False
2. True
3. False
4. True
5. False

Multiple Choice
6. d **7.** a **8.** d **9.** b

LESSON QUIZ 5-3
Matching
1. b **2.** c **3.** e **4.** a **5.** d
Multiple Choice
6. b **7.** c **8.** d **9.** a **10.** b

LESSON QUIZ 5-4
True/False
1. True
2. False
3. True
4. False
5. True

Multiple Choice
6. b **7.** b **8.** b **9.** a **10.** c

CHAPTER 5 TEST, TRADITIONAL

True/False

1. True
2. False
3. True
4. True
5. False

Matching

6. d 7. a 8. e 9. c 10. b

Multiple Choice

11. c 12. c 13. b 14. b 15. a
16. b 17. d 18. d 19. d

Short Answer

20. the Sugar Act

21. 1764–1767

22. Correct answers should include: taxes imposed on the colonies; armies sent in to occupy cities; soldiers being rude and violent to colonists; soldiers stealing from shops, fighting with people, and competing for jobs.

23. Correct answers should include: They could be ready to fight at a minute's notice.

Essay

24. Correct answers should include: The First Continental Congress drafted a statement of grievances calling for the repeal of 13 acts of Parliament passed since 1763. They declared that these laws violated the colonists' rights. The delegates also voted to boycott all British goods and trade and to arm themselves and form militias. They agreed to meet again if the British did not address their complaints. The Second Continental Congress authorized the printing of money and set up a post office. It established committees to communicate with Native Americans and with other countries. It also created the Continental Army to fight the battle against Britain in a more organized way than the colonial militias could.

CHAPTER 5 TEST, DOCUMENT-BASED QUESTIONS

Short Answer

1. to get money by collecting taxes on the colonists

2. because they did not think the taxes were fair

3. as a refuge from tyrants and persecution

4. Paine was a Patriot because he supported independence for the colonies.

5. Boston

6. The British troops battled with minutemen who came in from North Bridge, turned around, and headed back toward Boston.

Essay

7. Correct answers should include: After the French and Indian War, the British controlled most of North America, and they wanted to protect it. King George III issued the Proclamation of 1763, which banned colonists to live west of the Appalachian Mountains. He sent soldiers to reinforce this proclamation. Great Britain also had huge debts. British government imposed taxes on the colonists to help pay their debts. The Parliament passed acts like the Sugar Act and the Stamp Act. The colonists were angry about these acts and other acts because they believed they were unfair. They did not want to be taxed without their consent. As a result, colonists boycotted British goods and formed groups like the Sons of Liberty. When British troops were sent to colonial cities like Boston, there was violence. Colonists formed a political body called the Continental Congress to represent them and fight the British. They also formed militias. After many battles, colonists had to decide whether to be Loyalists or Patriots. The Second Continental Congress discussed whether to declare colonists independent or to keep them under British rule. A committee was chosen to draw up the Declaration of Independence.

CHAPTER 6
LESSON QUIZ 6-1
True/False

1. False
2. False
3. True
4. False
5. True

Multiple Choice

6. d   **7.** a   **8.** c   **9.** c   **10.** b

LESSON QUIZ 6-2
Completion
1. Saratoga
2. General George Washington
3. financial aid
4. taxes
5. slavery

Multiple Choice
6. c   **7.** b   **8.** d   **9.** b

LESSON QUIZ 6-3
True/False
1. True
2. False
3. True
4. True
5. False

Multiple Choice
6. b   **7.** a   **8.** b   **9.** d   **10.** c

LESSON QUIZ 6-4
Matching
1. b   **2.** c   **3.** e   **4.** a   **5.** d

Multiple Choice
6. d   **7.** b   **8.** c   **9.** b   **10.** d

CHAPTER 6 TEST, TRADITIONAL
True/False
1. False
2. True
3. False
4. False
5. False

Matching
6. a   **7.** d   **8.** b   **9.** e   **10.** c

Multiple Choice
11. c   **12.** d   **13.** d   **14.** c   **15.** c
16. d   **17.** d   **18.** b   **19.** b

Short Answer
20. hostile

21. the victory at Saratoga

22. Patriots

23. Correct answers should include: The bills quickly lost their value because the amount of bills in circulation grew faster than the supply of gold and silver backing them. This situation led to inflation.

Essay

24. Correct answers should include: The Patriots' advantages included fighting on their own ground; fighting for the freedom of their own land, which gave them an advantage over the hired Hessians of the British army; and their brilliant leader, George Washington. The Patriots' disadvantages included a small population; lack of a regular army or strong navy; lack of military experience; a short supply of weapons and ammunition; and a lack of agreement among American colonists, some of whom were either neutral or were Loyalists, not Patriots.

CHAPTER 6 TEST, DOCUMENT-BASED QUESTIONS
Short Answer
1. [General] Charles Cornwallis

2. British capture Savannah, 1778

3. Savannah, Charles Town, and Camden

4. movement of British forces

5. Yorktown

6. Correct answers should include: The soldiers were in surprisingly good-humor in very poor conditions.

7. Correct answers should include: discontented with his surroundings and longing for home.

8. Correct answers should include: fatigue, cold, sickness, starvation, poor clothing, poor food/cooking, hard lodging, smoke, bad weather.

Essay

9. Correct answers should include: The American army consisted mostly of American colonists, whereas the British army contained many Hessian mercenaries. While the American

colonists were fighting on their own soil for their country's freedom, the mercenaries in the British army had no personal stake in the outcome. They were fighting only for money.

CHAPTER 7
LESSON QUIZ 7-1
Modified True/False

1. False—By the END OF 1780, all states HAD STATE CONSTITUTIONS.
2. False—Americans were DETERMINED TO LIMIT the power in the hands of a single ruler.
3. True

Multiple Choice

4. a	**5.** b	**6.** c	**7.** b	**8.** d

LESSON QUIZ 7-2
Completion

1. depression
2. Shays's Rebellion
3. slavery
4. Constitutional Convention
5. 1808

Multiple Choice

6. b	**7.** b	**8.** d	**9.** a

LESSON QUIZ 7-3
Matching

1. c	**2.** a	**3.** d	**4.** e	**5.** b

Multiple Choice

6. d	**7.** d	**8.** d	**9.** b	**10.** c

CHAPTER 7 TEST, TRADITIONAL
True/False

1. True
2. False
3. False
4. True
5. False

Matching

6. c	**7.** a	**8.** e	**9.** b	**10.** d

Multiple Choice

11. c	**12.** d	**13.** b	**14.** a	**15.** b
16. b	**17.** d	**18.** c	**19.** c	**20.** b

Short Answer

21. Correct answers should include: to carry out the nation's laws and policies.

22. the national government

23. Correct answers should include: He believed that because of the importance given to the laws of the nation, the states' bills of rights were not enough protection for citizens without a national bill of rights.

24. Correct answers should include: Each state had one vote on all questions. Decisions were made based on a majority vote of all states present. The sessions were closed to the public so that the delegates could speak freely.

25. Correct answers should include: Slavery existed and was legal in every state. However, it was not a major source of labor in the North. Eventually, many groups there began working to end it. On the other hand, the plantation system of the South had grown to depend on the work of enslaved people. Many white Southerners feared that their economy could not survive without slavery. As Americans began to question how to strengthen the Articles of Confederation, these differences made those discussions more challenging.

CHAPTER 7 TEST, DOCUMENT-BASED QUESTIONS
Short Answer

1. Virginia; 292,627

2. 1,110

3. Virginia and New Hampshire

4. 399,721

5. Rhode Island and New Hampshire

6. In the Constitution written and discussed in 1789, Mason feels that the vast power of the Congress and its considerable expansion threatens available powers for the states. Moreover, people's individual rights are kept unprotected with no specific statement to ensure such rights.

He mentions the lack of protection for press freedom and the right to trial by jury, and points out the potential dangers of being armed in peacetime.

7. These actions included granting monopolies in business, establishing new crimes, inflicting unusual and severe punishments, and increasing the powers of Congress.

Essay

8. Correct answers should include: After the American Revolution, the United States needed a plan to govern the new nation. Eventually, states created a government plan called the Articles of Confederation. In response to its recent conflict with Great Britain, this plan formed a weak central government. The greatest powers were given to the individual states. However, after some time this weak government began to cause problems to the new nation. The leaders of the country realized that they needed to make changes to the government. After a great deal of debate, a new plan was developed. The Constitution of the United States created a more powerful central government. However, Constitutional Convention delegates worked for a system of checks and balances that prevented a part of the government from obtaining too much power. These changing ideas about government were related to the changing ideas about individual rights in the United States. The Framers of the Constitution drew on historical papers focusing on people's fundamental rights. Many delegates also called for including in the Constitution an additional Bill of Rights protecting individual liberties from governmental influence. During this period, enslaved people's rights also began to change. In the North, a growing number of African Americans started to recover their freedom. Questions about slavery in the United States would continue dividing the nation as the Constitution was developed.

CHAPTER 8
LESSON QUIZ 8-1
Completion

1. Bill of Rights
2. preamble to the Constitution
3. contradicts

4. (formerly enslaved) African Americans
5. implied powers

Multiple Choice

6. b   7. c   8. a   9. c

LESSON QUIZ 8-2
True/False

1. True
2. True
3. False
4. True
5. True

Multiple Choice

6. c   7. c   8. c   9. c   10. b

CHAPTER 8 TEST, TRADITIONAL
True/False

1. True
2. False
3. True
4. True
5. False

Matching

6. b   7. e   8. a   9. c   10. d

Multiple Choice

11. b   12. a   13. c   14. a   15. b
16. d   17. d   18. b   19. a   20. c

Short Answer

21. Correct answers should include: Immigrants must agree to accept the rights and responsibilities that go with citizenship.

22. We the People

23. Correct answers should include: Congress cannot create religions or stop people from practicing their religion; Congress cannot restrict free speech, freedom of the press, the right to gather peacefully, nor the right to make complaints to the government.

24. Bill of Rights

25. Correct responses should include: I do not think one branch of the government is more important than the others. The system of checks and

balances is in place because no one branch of the government is any more or less important than the others. For our government system to work, it is essential that all three branches of government work together.

CHAPTER 8 TEST, DOCUMENT-BASED QUESTIONS

Multiple Choice

1. b   **2.** c

Short Answer

3. checks and balances

4. Correct answers should include: The Constitution limits the actions of government by specifically listing powers it does and does not have.

5. Correct answers should include: The authority of the people; people are the source of the government's power.

6. Federalism

Essay

7. Correct answers should include: The U.S. government was formed to guarantee and protect the rights of the people. The federal government was created as a republic to allow the people to rule their own nation. The government was formed to create a democratic system where leaders are selected by voting. The U.S. government serves the people and provides for their needs.

CHAPTER 9

LESSON QUIZ 9-1

Multiple Choice

1. c   **2.** a   **3.** d   **4.** b   **5.** a

Short Answer

6. a tradition

7. the cabinet

8. Thomas Jefferson

9. the Judiciary Act of 1789

10. Correct answers should include: a person who risks money to make a profit.

LESSON QUIZ 9-2

Matching

1. b   **2.** d   **3.** a   **4.** e   **5.** c

Multiple Choice

6. d   **7.** c   **8.** c   **9.** b   **10.** b

LESSON QUIZ 9-3

Completion

1. political parties

2. Federalist

3. partisan

4. X, Y, and Z

5. Alien and Sedition

Multiple Choice

6. d   **7.** d   **8.** c   **9.** d   **10.** c

CHAPTER 9 TEST, TRADITIONAL

True/False

1. False

2. True

Multiple Choice

3. c   **4.** b   **5.** b   **6.** d   **7.** d

8. c   **9.** a   **10.** b   **11.** b   **12.** a

Short Answer

13. Shawnee chief Blue Jacket

14. Correct answers should include: It did not deal with the issue of impressments or British interference with American trade.

15. Correct answers should include: support the troops, pay public debt, regulate trade.

16. Correct answers should include: Congress cannot limit the freedom of speech.

17. Correct answers should include: In 1797 it was possible to elect a president and vice president from different parties because, under the provisions of the Constitution, the person with the second highest number of electoral votes became vice president, even though he might represent a party different from the elected president.

CHAPTER 9 TEST, DOCUMENT-BASED QUESTIONS

Short Answer

1. Correct answers should include: Washington says that the United States has done better with its second plan of government, the Constitution, than it did on its first try with the Articles of Confederation.

2. Correct answers should include: Washington notes that now the mutual interests of the states have been more closely brought together in a manageable system that includes providing for security and making changes ("amendment") when needed.

3. once

4. The Amendment provides exemptions for cases arising in the land or naval forces, in the Militia, or when in actual service in time of War or public danger.

5. Correct answers should include: It prevents the government from interpreting or using enumerated rights in the Constitution as a way to deny other rights to people.

6. Correct answers should include: The debt should not be undertaken without providing for sources of its repayment.

CHAPTER 10

LESSON QUIZ 10-1

Completion

1. John Adams
2. Twelfth Amendment
3. custom duties
4. national debt
5. midnight judges

Multiple Choice

6. d   7. a   8. c   9. c   10. c

LESSON QUIZ 10-2

True/False

1. False
2. True
3. True
4. True
5. False

Multiple Choice

6. d   7. b   8. c   9. d   10. b

LESSON QUIZ 10-3

True/False

1. True
2. False
3. True
4. True
5. True

Short Answer

6. Correct answers should include: Many French and British merchant ships remained at home to avoid being destroyed or captured by enemy ships. This allowed American shippers to increase trade.

7. Tripoli declared war on the United States in 1801.

8. Correct answers should include: A British warship, the *Leopard*, fired upon an American ship, the *Chesapeake*, killing three crew members.

9. Tecumseh

10. Henry Clay and John Calhoun

LESSON QUIZ 10-4

Matching

1. e   2. d   3. a   4. c   5. b

Multiple Choice

6. b   7. b   8. a   9. b   10. c

CHAPTER 10 TEST, TRADITIONAL

True/False

1. True
2. False
3. False
4. True
5. True

Matching

6. b   7. d   8. e   9. a   10. c

Multiple Choice

11. b	**12.** b	**13.** a	**14.** a	**15.** b
16. c	**17.** a	**18.** d	**19.** b	**20.** d

Short Answer

21. Correct answers should include: Alexander Hamilton was struck by a bullet and fell. Aaron Burr seemed to regret what happened.

22. Correct answers should include: Clark is very grateful for the help these Native Americans provide to the expedition as it moves through territory previously unknown to Europeans. He understands the importance of trade with such groups and is experienced and sensitive enough to know and/or to have brought along appropriate trade goods—in this instance, fish hooks.

23. Correct answers should include: Many Federalists opposed the purchase because they feared any new states created from the territory would be Republican. A group of Federalists in Massachusetts plotted to secede from the Union.

24. Correct answers should include: They sent hundreds of letters to leading citizens and newspapers to make their views public.

Essay

25. Correct answers should include: Outraged by the attack on the *Chesapeake*, Americans called for action against the British. President Thomas Jefferson and his supporters sought a course of action other than war—the Embargo Act. By using the embargo, Jefferson hoped to avoid war. The embargo wiped out American commerce. New England ships were stuck in their ports, which caused unemployment to rise. In the South, tobacco meant for Europe rotted on the docks and cotton went unpicked. In the West, the price of wheat declined and river traffic came to a halt.

CHAPTER 10 TEST, DOCUMENT-BASED QUESTIONS

Multiple Choice

1. a

Short Answer

2. Correct answers should include: He believes the Great Spirit gave the land to all Native Americans, and individual groups do not have the right to sell it.

3. Correct answers should include: The settlers are always pushing for more land.

4. Correct answers should include: because Native Americans had lived on it first.

Essay

5. Correct answers should include: Native Americans, led by the Shawnee chief Tecumseh, wanted to stop white settlers from moving farther into Native American lands. They formed a confederacy to unite the tribal nations against the white settlers and allied themselves with the British, who supplied the Native Americans with arms. At first these alliances slowed American progress in the war. But after Tecumseh was killed in the Battle of the Thames, these alliances ended. This allowed American forces to defeat the Creeks and take much of their land.

CHAPTER 11
LESSON QUIZ 11-1
True/False

1. True
2. False
3. True
4. True
5. False

Multiple Choice

6. b	**7.** c	**8.** a	**9.** d

LESSON QUIZ 11-2
Completion

1. 1790
2. Erie Canal
3. steam
4. locks
5. quilting and sewing

Multiple Choice

6. a	**7.** b	**8.** b	**9.** d

LESSON QUIZ 11-3
Matching

1. b	**2.** e	**3.** a	**4.** c	**5.** d

Answer Key *cont.*

Multiple Choice

6. a   **7.** d   **8.** b   **9.** c

CHAPTER 11 TEST, TRADITIONAL

True/False

1. False
2. True
3. False
4. False
5. False

Matching

6. c   **7.** a   **8.** e   **9.** b   **10.** d

Multiple Choice

11. d   **12.** b   **13.** a   **14.** b   **15.** d
16. c   **17.** a   **18.** a   **19.** a   **20.** b

Short Answer

21. President James Monroe

22. Lake Erie

23. Correct answers should include: Rivers enabled factories to have waterpower; goods could easily be shipped to markets along rivers.

24. Correct answers should include: It was a warning to European nations to keep out of North and South America.

Essay

25. Correct answers should include: The Industrial Revolution first appeared in the New England states because of New England's geography. New England's soil was poor, and farming was difficult. As a result, people were willing to leave their farms to find work elsewhere. New England had many rivers and streams that provided the waterpower necessary to run the machinery in the factories. New England's geographic location was also an advantage. New England had many shipping ports for the transportation of cotton and cloth bound for markets throughout the nation.

CHAPTER 11 TEST, DOCUMENT-BASED QUESTIONS

Short Answer

1. Genesee Road

2. Correct answers should include: to connect Ohio to Eastern states

3. better roads and canals

4. Correct answers should include: because transportation would be easier and cheaper than earlier

5. Correct answers should include: Raw materials from the South and the West could be easily shipped to the East and North for use in manufacturing, then shipped back to the South and West as manufactured goods.

Essay

6. Correct answers should include: Technology was changing the way people made goods, and this production occurred in factories. These changes began in the geographic area of New England. Infertile soil of New England forced people to look for jobs far from the farms and in factories. Many rivers and streams from New England supplied the waterpower needed to operate engines in factories. Besides, New England had a lot of ports, allowing barges to arrive and leave near areas to the factories.

CHAPTER 12

LESSON QUIZ 12-1

Matching

1. e   **2.** d   **3.** c   **4.** a   **5.** b

Multiple Choice

6. a   **7.** b   **8.** b   **9.** a   **10.** b

LESSON QUIZ 12-2

Completion

1. Jackson
2. Oklahoma
3. *Worcester* v. *Georgia*
4. Tears
5. African American

Multiple Choice

6. b   **7.** d   **8.** d   **9.** a   **10.** b

LESSON QUIZ 12-3

True/False

1. True
2. True
3. False
4. True
5. False

Discovering Our Past: A History of the United States

Copyright © McGraw-Hill Education. Permission is granted to reproduce for classroom use.

Multiple Choice

6. a   **7.** c   **8.** a   **9.** c

CHAPTER 12 TEST, TRADITIONAL

True/False

1. True

2. False

3. False

4. True

5. True

Matching

6. e   **7.** b   **8.** a   **9.** d   **10.** c

Multiple Choice

11. b   **12.** c   **13.** b   **14.** c   **15.** b

16. c   **17.** d   **18.** b

Short Answer

19. the North and the East

20. none

21. Democrats

22. Democrats

Essay

23. Correct answers should include: In the 1824 election, no candidate received a majority of electoral votes, so the House of Representatives was to select the president. Henry Clay, Speaker of the House, used his influence to help Adams become president. Once in office, Adams appointed Clay Secretary of State, traditionally the stepping-stone to the presidency. Andrew Jackson's supporters accused the two of making a "corrupt bargain" and stealing the election.

CHAPTER 12 TEST, DOCUMENT-BASED QUESTIONS

Multiple Choice

1. b

Short Answer

2. the Indian Removal Act

3. savage

4. as civilized Christians

5. Correct answers should include: They have refused to fit in with white Americans.

6. Correct answers should include: They will be wiped out.

7. Correct answers should include: as an act of kindness and generosity.

Essay

8. Correct answers should include: Many Native Americans had established peaceful farming communities. Settlers wanted the federal government to take Native American land from them and give it to the settlers. Jackson agreed that the Native Americans should be forced to move to the Great Plains. He pushed the Indian Removal Act through Congress. The Act forced Native Americans to sell their land and move west. The Cherokee went to court to fight the law. The Supreme Court ruled in favor of the Cherokee, but Jackson refused to comply. Instead, he forced some 15,000 Cherokee to relocate. Many died on this Trail of Tears.

CHAPTER 13

LESSON QUIZ 13-1

Matching

1. b   **2.** e   **3.** c   **4.** a   **5.** d

Multiple Choice

6. b   **7.** c   **8.** c   **9.** c   **10.** b

LESSON QUIZ 13-2

True/False

1. True

2. False

3. True

4. False

5. False

Multiple Choice

6. a   **7.** a   **8.** c   **9.** c   **10.** a

LESSON QUIZ 13-3

True/False

1. True

2. False

3. False

4. True

5. False

Multiple Choice

6. c   **7.** c   **8.** b   **9.** a

LESSON QUIZ 13-4

Completion

1. Californios
2. Gold Rush
3. Brigham Young
4. Sutter's Mill
5. vigilantes

Multiple Choice

6. a 7. b 8. b 9. a 10. d

CHAPTER 13 TEST, TRADITIONAL

True/False

1. False
2. True
3. True
4. False
5. True

Matching

6. a 7. b 8. d 9. c 10. e

Multiple Choice

11. a 12. a 13. c 14. c 15. d
16. b 17. a 18. b 19. d 20. b

Short Answer

21. Correct answers should include: President Jackson refused the request because Texas allowed slavery. Adding the territory to the United States would upset the balance of slave and free states in Congress, which could cause problems for the country.

22. Correct answers should include: Forty-niners were people looking for gold. They were called forty-niners because they arrived in California in 1849.

23. It made California more diverse, as people arrived from all over the world.

24. They were seeking safe haven, as disapproving neighbors forced them to move on.

Essay

25. Correct answers should include: At first, Mexico welcomed these newcomers because it wished to increase settlement. As more and more Americans moved to Texas, however, this changed. Americans soon outnumbered Tejanos.

They began to refuse to follow Mexico's rules, including learning Spanish and becoming Catholic. The Americans also brought slaves into Texas, which the Mexicans disliked. As a result of all these issues, Mexico issued a decree in 1830, closing its borders to further immigration.

CHAPTER 13 TEST, DOCUMENT-BASED QUESTIONS

Short Answer

1. Correct answers should include: According to the graph, he won the states of Connecticut, Maine, and New Hampshire.

2. Correct answers should include: James Polk won more states than Henry Clay. Polk won Connecticut, Maine, and New Hampshire, while Clay won Massachusetts and Vermont.

3. Massachusetts; Whig candidate, about 70,000; Democratic candidate, about 55,000

4. Correct answers should include: Some mountain men were employed and paid by trading companies, while others, called freemen, worked for themselves.

5. Correct answers should include: Mountain men hunted in the wild and had to face challenges like steep rocks and fast streams. Attacks by Native Americans were also common.

6. Correct answers should include: Mountain men worked for wages or for themselves. They were persistent and brave, willing to climb rocks and go through streams in difficult circumstances. Sometimes they fell victim to Native Americans.

CHAPTER 14

LESSON QUIZ 14-1

True/False

1. True
2. True
3. True
4. False
5. False

Multiple Choice

6. a 7. c 8. d 9. c 10. b

LESSON QUIZ 14-2
Matching
  1. a   **2.** d   **3.** c   **4.** e   **5.** b
Multiple Choice
  6. b   **7.** a   **8.** a   **9.** b   **10.** c

LESSON QUIZ 14-3
Completion
  1. slavery
  2. industry
  3. 50 times
  4. land
  5. South

Multiple Choice
  6. b   **7.** c   **8.** a   **9.** c   **10.** d

LESSON QUIZ 14-4
Matching
  1. c   **2.** e   **3.** d   **4.** a   **5.** b
Multiple Choice
  6. d   **7.** c   **8.** d   **9.** c   **10.** d

CHAPTER 14 TEST, TRADITIONAL
True/False
  1. True
  2. True
  3. True
  4. False
  5. False

Matching
  6. e   **7.** b   **8.** a   **9.** d   **10.** c
Multiple Choice
  11. c   **12.** b   **13.** d   **14.** b   **15.** d
  16. d   **17.** c   **18.** b   **19.** c

Short Answer
  20. Correct answers should include: on-the-job accidents.

  21. Correct answers should include: The South had few people per square mile. Many families could not send their children great distances to attend school. In addition, many Southerners believed education was a private matter, not a state function.

Essay
  22. Correct answers should include: The economy of the South depended on slave labor. As the demand for cotton grew, Southern farmers and plantation owners wanted to produce more cotton. Having more enslaved workers enabled Southern cotton growers to increase cotton production. The invention of the cotton gin encouraged Southern farmers to grow even more cotton. The domestic slave trade became a big business as the demand for cotton continued to grow with increased industrialization.

CHAPTER 14 TEST, DOCUMENT-BASED QUESTIONS
Short Answer
  1. 1850

  2. 16%

  3. Ireland

  4. Correct answers should include: This excerpt emphasizes the very long hours and exhausting work that had to be put in each day by enslaved people on cotton plantations.

  5. Correct answers should include: This excerpt tells that field hands must work from first daylight until late at night, sometimes even until the middle of the night.

  6. Correct answers should include: Field hands were not allowed to rest or stop work until nightfall.

Essay
  7. Correct answers should include: Because farming was so profitable with the boom in cotton, Southern farmers remained committed to farming, rather than starting new businesses. Another stumbling block was the lack of capital to invest in businesses. Wealthy Southerners had their wealth invested in land and enslaved laborers. Planters would have had to sell enslaved laborers to raise the money to build factories. In addition, the market for manufactured goods in the South was smaller than it was in the North because a large portion of the Southern population consisted of

enslaved people with no money to buy merchandise. Also, some Southerners simply did not want industry to flourish there and preferred to maintain a largely agricultural economy.

CHAPTER 15
LESSON QUIZ 15-1
True/False

1. True
2. False
3. True
4. False
5. True

Multiple Choice

6. d   7. d   8. a   9. d   10. d

LESSON QUIZ 15-2
True/False

1. False
2. True
3. True
4. False
5. True

Multiple Choice

6. d   7. b   8. b   9. c

LESSON QUIZ 15-3
Multiple Choice

1. b   2. a   3. b   4. b   5. a

Short Answer

6. Correct answers should include: the right to vote.

7. Declaration of Sentiments and Resolutions

8. Susan B. Anthony

9. Mount Holyoke Female Seminary

10. Wyoming

CHAPTER 15 TEST, TRADITIONAL
True/False

1. False
2. False
3. True

4. True
5. False

Matching

6. c   7. a   8. e   9. b   10. d

Multiple Choice

11. a   12. c   13. a   14. a   15. b
16. b   17. d   18. d   19. d   20. c

Short Answer

21. Second Great Awakening

22. visually impaired

23. Correct answers should include: Harriet Tubman looks at her hands because she feels so different as a free person that she wants to make sure she is still herself. She says she feels as though she has gone to heaven. Because her hands are close and familiar parts of herself, parts that she knows well, looking at them can reassure her she remains the same person.

24. Correct answers should include: Whittier feels sympathetic toward women and enslaved people. He thinks women should join the movement to end slavery.

Essay

25. Correct answers should include: The women's movement was focused on gaining greater equality between women and men. Women organized to fight for the right to vote. They also wanted to be allowed to enter professions that were previously only for men. The antislavery movement was focused on the abolition of slavery for African Americans. The two movements were linked by their shared goal of equality for all people. Women such as Lucretia Mott were active in both the women's movement and abolition.

CHAPTER 15 TEST, DOCUMENT-BASED QUESTIONS
Short Answer

1. abolition of slavery

2. Correct answers should include: They reacted violently. Garrison had to be jailed to protect him from an angry mob.

3. Correct answers should include: The Fourth of July is a celebration of liberty, but this liberty does not apply to enslaved people.

4. The American Colonization Society

5. Monrovia

6. 12,000–15,000

Essay

7. Correct answers should include: Abolitionists in the North believed slavery was a moral wrong. They argued slavery should be abolished to uphold American ideals of liberty and justice. Some early abolitionists wanted to establish a colony in Africa for formerly enslaved people. Other Northerners saw the antislavery movement as a threat to the nation's social order. They believed that once freed, the African Americans could never blend into American society. They also feared the abolitionists could begin a war between the North and South. Others feared they would lose their jobs to those who would move to the North and work for cheaper wages.

CHAPTER 16
LESSON QUIZ 16-1
Matching

1. b 2. e 3. d 4. a 5. c

Multiple Choice

6. b 7. c 8. b 9. b 10. a

LESSON QUIZ 16-2
True/False

1. True
2. True
3. False
4. True
5. False

Multiple Choice

6. d 7. a 8. b 9. c 10. b

LESSON QUIZ 16-3
Completion

1. slavery

2. three

3. populous
4. Republican
5. secession

Multiple Choice

6. d 7. b 8. d 9. b 10. a

CHAPTER 16 TEST, TRADITIONAL
True/False

1. False
2. True
3. False
4. True
5. True

Matching

6. e 7. b 8. c 9. d 10. a

Multiple Choice

11. a 12. c 13. d 14. c 15. b
16. c 17. a 18. b 19. c 20. c

Short Answer

21. Correct answers should include: It increased their opposition to slavery.

22. Correct answers should include: by breaking them.

23. three

24. 1824, 1832, 1844

Essay

25. Correct answers should include: The North was industrial and the South agricultural. Slavery was far more prevalent in the South than in the North. A growing number of Northerners wanted to restrict or end slavery. Southerners felt that Northerners had no real economic stake in slavery and little to lose by its abolition. Even Southerners who disliked slavery resented Northern interference in their affairs. Both Southerners and Northerners became attached to the views common in their regions, and this exaggerated loyalty to their part of the country led to conflict.

CHAPTER 16 TEST, DOCUMENT-BASED QUESTIONS
Short Answer

1. Douglas received the fewest electoral votes.

2. Lincoln received the largest portion of the popular vote.

3. Douglas had the greatest percentage increase.

4. Bell received the smallest portion of the popular vote.

5. Breckinridge won in the southern United States.

6. New York had the most electoral votes at 35.

7. Lincoln won more than half the electoral votes.

8. Answers will vary, but students should acknowledge that the split in the Democratic Party helped Lincoln win. If there had been only one Democratic candidate, then that candidate would have received a greater portion of the votes split between Douglas and Breckinridge.

Essay

9. Correct answers should include: The 1860 election set the stage for the Civil War. Lincoln represented the Republican Party, who did not want to end slavery but also did not want it to spread. Southern whites, who relied on slave labor to run their farms and plantations, were afraid that a Republican victory would threaten slavery in the South. Northerners, who were mostly anti-slavery, supported Lincoln because they also thought his election would move the country toward abolishing slavery. Many Southern states did not put Lincoln's name on their voting ballots, but all the Northern states did, and there were so many more voters in the North than the South that Lincoln was elected. After the election, Southern states started leaving the Union. The Civil War soon followed.

CHAPTER 17
LESSON QUIZ 17-1
True/False

1. True
2. False
3. False
4. False
5. True

Multiple Choice

6. c   7. a   8. b   9. b

LESSON QUIZ 17-2
Completion

1. George B. McClellan
2. defend or protect
3. *Virginia*
4. New Orleans

Multiple Choice

5. b   6. d   7. c   8. d

LESSON QUIZ 17-3
Matching

1. e   2. c   3. a   4. b   5. d

Multiple Choice

6. b   7. c   8. b   9. a

LESSON QUIZ 17-4
True/False

1. False
2. True
3. False
4. True
5. False

Multiple Choice

6. a   7. d   8. a   9. b

LESSON QUIZ 17-5
Completion

1. General Ulysses S. Grant
2. George B. McClellan
3. 1865
4. individual states

Multiple Choice

5. d   6. c   7. d   8. a

CHAPTER 17 TEST, TRADITIONAL
True/False

1. True
2. True
3. False
4. False
5. True

Matching

6. b   **7.** e   **8.** a   **9.** c   **10.** d

Multiple Choice

11. d   **12.** a   **13.** a   **14.** a   **15.** b

16. d   **17.** d   **18.** d   **19.** c

Short Answer

20. the Battle of Antietam

21. Correct answers include: The character realizes that he might run away in a battle, he has "panic-fear" in his mind. He thinks about the consequences of fighting in a battle.

22. Correct answers include: Maryland was close to Richmond, the Confederate capital. Washington, D.C., was bordered by Maryland and Virginia, and if Maryland seceded, the Union government would be surrounded.

23. It was the most distinguished African American regiment in the Union army.

Essay

24. Correct answers should include: Although Lincoln hated slavery, he was at first reluctant to move against it because of the border states. Northerners such as Horace Greeley and Frederick Douglass asked Lincoln to make the war a fight to end slavery. Greeley and Douglass made several arguments to support ending slavery. They pointed out that it was morally wrong, and that it was the root of the division between North and South. They also believed that casting the war as a fight for freedom would convince antislavery nations like Britain and France not to support the Confederates.

CHAPTER 17 TEST, DOCUMENT-BASED QUESTIONS

Short Answer

1. Virginia

2. A Union victory (Grant drove Lee's army out of the city)

3. Correct answers include: Lunt is angry and anxious. The Yankees have taken or destroyed everything as they have moved through the South. The civilians left behind have nothing to eat, and all of their basic belongings such as blankets and clothes have been taken.

4. Correct answers include: The war left people without their belongings and food. The war also destroyed a large amount of property in the South.

5. the North

6. cotton; Britain and France

Essay

7. Correct answers include: The North had a larger population than the South. They also had more resources, such as railroads, exports, and manufactured goods. The North wanted to restore the Union. To do so, the North had to invade the South. Northerners did not believe that the South would be able to hold out against the greater resources of the North.

The South had excellent military leaders, as well as a strong fighting spirit. Most of the war was fought in the South, so the soldiers knew the land. The South conducted a defensive war so it could hold as much territory as possible. The South wanted to be an independent nation, the Confederate States of America. The South did not have to invade the North to achieve independence; it just needed to fight long and hard enough until the North was convinced that the war was not worth the cost.

CHAPTER 18

LESSON QUIZ 18-1

Matching

1. d   **2.** c   **3.** a   **4.** e   **5.** b

Multiple Choice

6. c   **7.** d   **8.** a   **9.** a   **10.** b

LESSON QUIZ 18-2

Completion

1. Black codes

2. Civil Rights Act

3. override

4. African Americans

5. Tenure of Office

Multiple Choice

6. c   **7.** b   **8.** d   **9.** b

LESSON QUIZ 18-3

True/False

1. True
2. False
3. False
4. True
5. True

Multiple Choice

6. d 7. a 8. c 9. c 10. d

LESSON QUIZ 18-4

Matching

1. e 2. c 3. a 4. b 5. d

Multiple Choice

6. b 7. c 8. d 9. b 10. c

CHAPTER 18 TEST, TRADITIONAL

True/False

1. False
2. False
3. False
4. True
5. True

Matching

6. e 7. d 8. b 9. a 10. c

Multiple Choice

11. c 12. d 13. b 14. c 15. d

16. a 17. c 18. d 19. b 20. a

Short Answer

21. South Carolina and Georgia

22. 1871

23. 1871 through 1875 (1871 through 1876 is acceptable.)

24. South Carolina

25. Correct answers should include: A majority of the state's white males had to swear loyalty to the Union. Only white males who swore they had not fought against the Union could vote for delegates to a state constitutional convention. Any new state constitution had to ban slavery. Former Confederates could not hold office.

CHAPTER 18 TEST, DOCUMENT-BASED QUESTIONS

Multiple Choice

1. b

Short Answer

2. three

3. about 10 years

4. between "First Reconstruction Act passed" and "Fifteenth Amendment ratified"

5. the Grant Administration

6. the beginning of the Hayes Administration

7. Hayes and Garfield

8. Correct answers should include: Because of charges of corruption in the Grant administration and an economic depression, Democrats (who did not support civil rights legislation) gained seats in the Senate and won control of the House of Representatives from the Republicans. The increased power of Democrats in Congress meant less commitment to Reconstruction and less support for African American rights.